ASHE Higher Education Report: Volume 37, Number 3
Kelly Ward, Lisa E. Wolf-Wendel, Series Editors

Veterans in Higher Education: When Johnny and Jane Come Marching to Campus

David DiRamio

Kathryn Jarvis

Veterans in Higher Education: When Johnny and Jane Come Marching to Campus
David DiRamio and Kathryn Jarvis
ASHE Higher Education Report: Volume 37, Number 3
Kelly Ward, Lisa E. Wolf-Wendel, Series Editors

ISSN 1551-6970   electronic ISSN 1554-6306   ISBN 978-1-1181-5079-5

The ASHE Higher Education Report is part of the Jossey-Bass Higher and Adult
Education Series and is published six times a year by Wiley Subscription Services,
Inc., A Wiley Company, at Jossey-Bass, 989 Market Street, San Francisco,
California 94103-1741.

For subscription information, see the Back Issue/Subscription Order Form
in the back of this volume.

CALL FOR PROPOSALS: Prospective authors are strongly encouraged to contact
Kelly Ward (kaward@wsu.edu) or Lisa Wolf-Wendel (lwolf@ku.edu). See "About
the ASHE Higher Education Report Series" in the back of this volume.

Visit the Jossey-Bass Web site at **www.josseybass.com.**

Printed in the United States of America on acid-free recycled paper.

The ASHE Higher Education Report is indexed in CIJE: Current Index to Jour-
nals in Education (ERIC), Current Abstracts (EBSCO), Education Index/Abstracts
(H.W. Wilson), ERIC Database (Education Resources Information Center),
Higher Education Abstracts (Claremont Graduate University), IBR & IBZ: Inter-
national Bibliographies of Periodical Literature (K.G. Saur), and Resources in
Education (ERIC).

Advisory Board

The ASHE Higher Education Report Series is sponsored by the Association for the Study of Higher Education (ASHE), which provides an editorial advisory board of ASHE members.

Contents

Executive Summary

According to an American Council on Education report in 2008, as many as 2 million students with military experience will take advantage of their education benefits and attend postsecondary institutions in all sectors of higher education during this decade. This "nontraditional" population, known as student veterans, includes those who have exited the armed services and those who still have military ties. They bring life experiences that few traditional-age students or, for that matter, faculty members, campus staff, or administrators can relate to or claim for themselves. These men and women are veterans of the wars in Iraq and Afghanistan, and many of them have faced war-related trauma—fierce combat, roadside bomb explosions, physical or psychological injuries, and the deaths of their comrades. As this unique population of students continues to grow on campuses across the nation, professionals in higher education, including those serving in central administration, academic affairs, and student affairs, are increasingly interested in understanding more about these students and helping them succeed.

Higher education has a rich history of assisting special populations such as first-generation attendees, minorities, and students with disabilities in achieving academic success. Following World War II, record numbers of war veterans enrolled in colleges and universities using educational benefits from the original GI bill. The impact that millions of new college students had on American higher education was unprecedented, and tremendous growth in postsecondary institutions occurred during that era. Today, generous benefits associated with the post-9/11 GI bill make attending college after war service an attractive option. The all-volunteer, modern military looks much different from what it did after World War II. Women account for more than one in seven service members, and because of advances in technology and medical care, the number of veterans who have survived physical trauma has increased dramatically. How can campus personnel best assist these students? One place to start is to familiarize oneself with the issues student veterans face.

This volume is intended to provide useful information about students with military experience who are attending college by blending the theoretical, practical, and empirical. We use some of the best-known theories and research in the literature on higher education as comfortable starting points from which to investigate the phenomenon of the veteran attending college. For example, we call upon Astin's well known I-E-O research framework as a tool for describing inputs, environmental factors, and outcomes associated with student veterans. This approach is particularly useful when considering Astin's findings on peer interactions and the strong peer bond that many students with military experience have as well as the types of supports that institutions can provide as positive environmental factors. Astin also provides a brief commentary on the topic.

Throughout this monograph, other frameworks and theories, particularly from the literature on college student development, from recognizable names such as Baxter Magolda, Braxton, Chickering, Schlossberg, and Tinto, are used. In some instances, we contacted the major theorists themselves, and they generously contributed their thoughts about student veterans. In other chapters, experts who have written on the subtopics presented in the chapters offered their ideas in areas such as persistence and departure, student development, and women's issues. The expert contributions strengthen the information provided for the reader and are to be used to integrate student development theory in planning programs and services for this population.

To inform the reader, we draw from the first "wave" of research on this topic of college students with military experience, much of it conducted over the past five years or so since 2007. Most of the work published in that period is qualitative, including research from the authors of this monograph. One report, *From Soldier to Student: Easing the Transition of Service Members on Campus*, published by the American Council on Education in 2009 and featured in this volume, is one of a few larger-scale, quantitative research projects to date and provides findings at the institutional level. Ultimately, we hope this book will inform the next wave of research, particularly longitudinal studies of persistence and student success, which are now possible as veterans matriculate year by year on their collegiate journeys.

Information about contemporary issues and best practices is addressed throughout the pages of this publication. For example, ideas about providing transition assistance and courses designed to help student veterans deal with the future (and the past) are presented. We introduce the reader to a unique subpopulation of women veterans and reveal some of the challenges they face, including military sexual trauma and higher rates of posttraumatic stress disorder than their male counterparts. Moreover, the latest statistics about how many of our military men and women have physical disabilities, invisible psychological injuries, or both, are alarming, and we raise questions about how prepared campus disabilities offices and counseling centers are for the increased numbers of student veterans who will require accommodations and assistance.

Drawing from information provided in this monograph and other sources, higher education professionals who possess a fundamental understanding of the issues faced by the student veteran population can provide sorely needed assistance in the transition to college, persistence at the institution, and degree attainment.

Foreword

Just this morning I awoke to NPR coverage of "soldiers coming home" to Pendelton, Oregon, after 400 days in Afghanistan. The story highlighted the transition to home and the many paths people take after serving in the military. One of these paths is to higher education. In many ways these students are just like any other—eager to learn, looking for next steps, and wanting to prepare for the future—and in other ways they are quite different. They tend to be older and based on their military background these students have a significant amount of worldly experience—some of which can have been quite traumatic. Many student veterans face challenges with the transition back to their families, U.S. culture, and into higher education. Often challenges colleges and universities and their staff are ill-equipped to address. While many campuses have some type of veterans programs and military support services, faculty and administrators are often at a loss when it comes to meeting the needs of student veterans. Students with military experience often have a background that is distinct from other student groups. Campus personnel want to do the right thing to help facilitate the transition and success of students with a military background, but it's not always clear what the right thing is.

David DiRamio and Kathryn Jarvis in this monograph, *Veterans in Higher Education: When Johnny and Jane Come Marching to Campus,* provide some of the necessary background and information colleges and universities can use in their work with student veterans. The monograph draws upon practical, theoretical, and empirical literature about students with military experience to provide readers with comprehensive and thought-provoking information. The authors take an interesting standpoint by merging theory and practice in their presentation of information. The manuscript goes beyond mere description of students or best practices, by drawing upon different areas of student development theory to provide a foundation for working with veteran students.

The monograph offers a very unique approach by not only using the literature and research generated by student development scholars such as Nancy Schlossberg, Alexander Astin, Vince Tinto, Linda Reisser, Margaret Baechtold, John Braxton, and Marcia Baxter-Magolda, the authors also talked with these scholars as a way to gain insight for how to use particular theories with veteran student populations. The personal approach to link theory and practice provides the readers with the opportunity to hear personally from scholars and how they see their theories applied to particular students. This approach is not only helpful to think in new and different ways about veteran students it is also a unique vantage point to see links between theory and practice. Often researchers and practitioners make links between different theoretical perspectives and particular areas of practice or to particular group of students, but the conversation takes place metaphorically between texts. The presentation in this monograph is unique in that readers hear personally from the theorist and how their particular strand of theoretical work can be applied to better meet the needs of veteran students even though much of the student development research has not been applied to veteran student populations. Hearing from the theorists directly helps the readers think critically about how theory can be used to inform practice. It's easy for student affairs practitioners to overlook theory in their every day work because they don't see the relevance or they are not sure of how to make connections. DiRamio and Jarvis help readers see how to make the connections by using different areas of literature and by having those who generate the research provide commentary.

The authors have been very comprehensive in their approach to the topic of veteran students They provide sufficient historical information to guide readers in addition to looking at the transition of veteran students to higher education, peer interactions and the campus environment, veteran student persistence, identity development for veteran students, and self authorship and curriculum. In addition the authors address issues associated with gender, an increasing area of interest, and provide an overview of institutional responses to student veterans. The book is comprehensive in its synthesis and analysis of current literature and practice.

As colleges and universities strive to address the needs of students with military experience, DiRamio and Jarvis's work provides important and useful information about student veterans. They provide readers not just with a list of best practices; they more importantly prompt their audience to think creatively about how to use what we know about students in general and how our best understanding of students can be used to aid the transition, learning, development, and success of student veterans.

Kelly Ward
Series Editor

Acknowledgments

We are so fortunate to have input from a number of colleagues and particularly want to thank the expert scholars or old friends, Alexander Astin, Margaret Baechtold, Marcia Baxter Magolda, John Braxton, Linda Reisser, and Nancy Schlossberg, who graciously offered insights and commentary about theory and practice as they relate to the population of student veterans.

We are especially grateful for the helpful comments and support offered by Kelly Ward and our reviewers. Their careful reading and suggestions have helped make the manuscript stronger.

Our work has been fueled by the tenacity and passionate struggles of many of the student veterans who will persevere and find their way as they strive to achieve the goal of a college degree. We hope this volume will aid administrators, student affairs personnel, faculty, advisors, and others as they welcome these men and women to the academy.

David DiRamio thanks Penny Barnes for proofreading and editorial advice but, more important, for her dedication and support. He also praises Roberta DiRamio, his mother, for a lifetime of love.

Kathryn Jarvis wishes to thank her colleagues for their endless support, candor, and willingness to listen to what she thinks, just one more time. She also wants to give kudos to her father's still fine-tuned editorial skill at ninety-two years and his unerring ability to let her know when she might want to phrase it differently. And, of course, to Lucy, Jake, and John, who still make her laugh.

Published online in Wiley Online Library
(wileyonlinelibrary.com) • DOI: 10.1002/aehe.3703

Old Friends and New Faces

A POPULATION OF STUDENTS is emerging on college campuses across the nation. In some ways they are just like other college students, particularly those considered "nontraditional" such as transfer students and adult learners. In other respects, however, they possess unique characteristics stemming from personal experiences that few college administrators, faculty members, campus staff, or traditionally aged students can claim for themselves or, perhaps, empathize with and relate to. The group we are referring to are students with military experience, including those who have served on combat duty in the wars in Iraq and Afghanistan. Student veterans—those who have exited the armed services and those who still have military ties—are entering colleges and universities in increasing numbers. If you have not noticed them on your campus, it is likely you will (and soon). Thanks in part to generous educational benefits earned while serving their country, they are indeed coming to higher education, perhaps as many as 2 million students in the near term (American Council on Education, 2008). Are we, the higher education community, including those of us in central administration, academic affairs, and student affairs, ready to welcome student veterans into postsecondary education and assist them in achieving success?

This volume is intended to provide useful information about students with military experience who are attending college by blending the theoretical, practical, and empirical. As student veterans, like typical college students, navigate through the academic system, the challenges faced can be better understood if we can adapt and integrate student development theory in planning programs and services for this population. The "old friends" referred to in this introduction include some of the best-known theorists and theories in the literature on higher education. Iconic names such as Astin, Baxter Magolda, Braxton, Chickering, Schlossberg, and Tinto (and others) provide a comfortable starting point from which to investigate the phenomenon of veterans attending college. In some cases, we contacted the major theorists themselves, who generously contributed their thoughts on the topic. In other instances, experts who have written on the subtopics presented in the chapters offered their ideas in areas such as persistence and departure, student development, and women's issues. Each contributor was initially contacted by telephone or e-mail and asked to provide his or her thoughts on the topic of student veterans, with some guiding questions provided to initiate the process. The idea behind our requests for expert contributions was to strengthen the information provided with additional input from prominent authors who are familiar names from the higher education literature. Readers trained in college administration and student development should find this "old friends" approach helpful as they consider the "new faces," the students themselves.

Many of these men and women who courageously served during times of conflict are now turning their attention toward postsecondary pursuits, and it is important that we as a nation, and the higher education community in particular, make reasonable efforts to provide the necessary supports to assist veterans in their collegiate journey. Higher education has a rich history of assisting special populations to achieve academic success, including minorities, first-generation attendees, and students with disabilities. And although each generation has its own story and distinct qualities, the phenomenon of the returning veteran is not an unfamiliar scenario in the history of the United States.

Following World War II, record numbers of war veterans enrolled in colleges and universities using educational benefits from the Servicemen's Readjustment Act of 1944, familiar to most readers as the GI bill. The impact that millions of new college students had on American higher education was unprecedented, and postsecondary education grew tremendously during that era. Interestingly, although many of us who work in higher education have no military experience and perhaps cannot relate to today's student veterans, most of us can venture back in our family histories to see where members of our own families served during past periods of conflict. In many cases, the trajectory of the family tree was altered for the better as a result of post–World War II college attendance by an elder. For many professors and senior administrators today, it is probable that college was not initially part of their family's tradition until a parent or grandparent attended college on the GI bill, subsequently paving the way for later generations and perhaps their own college education. Fast forward to the current generation, and one might wonder whether life paths are being similarly altered by contemporary war service, subsequent college attendance using educational benefits, and, ultimately, degree attainment in the twenty-first century. Surely they are! Moreover, perhaps we are witnessing the origins of a new "greatest generation" (Brokaw, 1998), as our servicemen and -women protect our freedoms in a world where terroristic extremism is once again a threat. If predictions made by sociologists Strauss and Howe (1991, 2000) are accurate, then this current generation, the Millennials (born in the period from 1982 to 2002), should emulate their "elder" generation, the post–World War II age group. A new generation of college-trained adults who have sacrificed much for their country could be what America needs in terms of leadership in this new millennium of rapid global change. Employers seem to think so, as we witness many corporations in the Fortune 500 instituting efforts to recruit the best and brightest from the military to management positions. But for the time being, let us go back to campus.

The following chapters contain theories, frameworks, facts, and ideas for consideration when approaching the subject of the newest generation of college students who have experienced military service. This information should be particularly useful for those whose task is to provide support and services for student veterans, including campus administrators and policymakers. Not much research has been conducted in this area to date, and most of the work published in the last five years is qualitative, including publications from the authors of this volume. We are just now beginning to see an increase in the number of publications about veterans in college, using both qualitative and quantitative methods, a few ambitious research projects currently under way, and substantial interest from graduate students writing dissertations. We hope this volume proves to be a catalyst for increased attention and awareness.

The next chapter, "Home Alone? Applying Theories of Transition to Support Student Veterans' Success," uses the lens of the transition process as a basis for contemplating the experience of student veterans. Theories from Schlossberg, Bridges, Wapner, and others provide the foundation for an adapted model for helping professionals in higher education who work with students who are transitioning from military service to college and civilian life. Transitions of this type often involve adjustments in a variety of areas, including personal, academic, vocational, and social. Institutional assistance is integral to aid students in transition, with a holistic approach preferred. Nancy Schlossberg provided us a thoughtful commentary, giving her insights about transition for these students.

In "What Matters to Veterans? Peer Influences and the Campus Environment," Astin's I–E–O model provides a framework for characterizing the importance of veterans' connecting with other veterans, which the research indicates may be vital for initial success and persistence when starting college. Veterans of war share a unique bond, and those ties can be useful when navigating the confusion and bureaucracy inherent in any college or university. It can occur in the student organization for veterans on campus or, more informally, in direct peer-to-peer interaction inside and outside the classroom. Moreover, the campus environment, as Astin made clear in his research and writings, plays a key role in this discussion and includes the programs and services designed to assist student veterans. Alexander Astin shared his thoughts in a brief commentary on the topic.

"Transition 2.0: Using Tinto's Model to Understand Student Veterans' Persistence" looks further into the collegiate journey of veterans, later into the matriculation process, and beyond initial peer connections to consider the interactions these students will have with the broader campus community, including faculty members and nonmilitary students. We consider Tinto's ideas about integration, both academic and social, and whether those concepts apply to older, experienced students. We ask how all of these factors may play into a student's decision to depart the institution or to persist. We also introduce two novel thoughts for readers to consider. First, we suggest that a veteran's transition from military duty to civilian college student is really not complete until interaction with diverse others takes place. Second, we put forward evidence that employers want a "civilian version" of the desirable military traits that veterans possess. John Braxton, renowned professor and higher education researcher, shares his thinking on the topics of persistence and departure related to student veterans.

"Crisis of Identity? Veteran, Civilian, Student" reviews some of the key literature on college student development, drawing from the seminal works of Chickering, Jossleson, Kegan, Perry, and others. A typological model for understanding identity development in student veterans is revealed based on Marcia's writings about identity formation and Jones and McEwen's theory of multiple dimensions of identity. This chapter provides a novel approach for considering where a student veteran is in terms of development and offers ideas about how to proceed toward a fulfilled civilian identity. This information should be helpful for those whose task is to create programs and services for students with military experience. Linda Reisser, coauthor with Arthur Chickering of *Education and Identity* (1993; featuring the seven vectors of student development), provides her ideas about student veterans.

"Women Warriors: Supporting Female Student Veterans" shows the reader a new wrinkle in the story of student veterans: females with military experience, including those who have experienced combat and other traumas. This chapter introduces a distinctive subpopulation of women on our campuses and reveals some of the challenges they face. For example, military sexual trauma is a big issue in the armed forces, and many women also suffer post-traumatic stress disorder (PTSD) at higher rates than men. One in seven military personnel is female, and information in this chapter confirms that many women serve in harm's way along with men. Today's version of warfare has no front lines of battle for women to stay behind. The issue of providing support specifically for women veterans is finally garnering more attention, and we hope this chapter inspires the higher education community to do its part to help. Margaret Baechtold, retired Air Force officer and director of Indiana University–Bloomington's center for veterans, offers her commentary about the phenomenon of female college students with military experience.

"Ideas for a Self-Authorship Curriculum for Students with Military Experience" draws heavily from the research of Baxter Magolda, Pizzalato, and others to conceive of ways in which a course for veterans can help in their transition to college. More than a traditional orientation class, this proposed curriculum includes reflective writing about experiences in war and college, challenges students to make meaning of those experiences, and introduces them to the concept of self-authoring one's own life. The tenets of self-authorship are ideal for older students who are transitioning to college and civilian life from an environment where heavy reliance on an external authority, the military way, is obligatory. Marcia Baxter Magolda provided insightful commentary on the topic.

"Institutional Response to an Emerging Population of Veterans" provides the types of empirical evidence and inferential analyses needed for data-driven decision making by senior administrators and policymakers. Using data from the American Council on Education's *From Soldier to Student* (Cook and Kim, 2009), we performed a secondary analysis, including a factor analysis, which revealed five areas for policy consideration, and explored differences in veteran services and support by educational sector and percentage of enrollment of veteran students. Quantitative research on students with military experience is lacking, particularly in terms of scale and sample size, and we trust this chapter helps fill a gap in the research literature.

The British historian and statesman James Bryce said, "The worth of a book is to be measured by what you can carry away from it" (Seaman, 2006, p. 44), and we hope you carry much with you from reading this volume. Carry with you some compassion for the men and women who have served our country so admirably, balanced with a fair sense of pragmatism about how much colleges and universities can do to support their success. Most important, we hope this volume inspires a wave of new research in this important topic.

Home Alone? Applying Theories of Transition to Support Student Veterans' Success

THE TRANSITION FROM MILITARY SERVICE to civilian life can be one of the most challenging encountered by any individual (Gettleman, 2005; Hoge, 2010). Researchers in one study found that "many veterans could not identify with society in general—as one succinctly stated, 'Out in society, there is a disconnection'" (Brenner and others, 2008, p. 219). This type of transition typically calls for adjustments in a variety of areas, including personal, social, academic, and vocational. Students with military experience present a special challenge for colleges and universities, not only because of their increasing numbers but also because of their differences from traditionally aged students and their unique characteristics associated with military experiences.

The Academy Award–winning motion picture *The Hurt Locker* (Bigelow, 2008) explored the devastating effect of repeated exposure to high-intensity combat situations on the members of an Army Explosive Ordnance Disposal team in Iraq. Army Staff Sergeant William James, played by Jeremy Renner, provided poignant examples of the difficulties experienced in transition to the civilian world from military service and combat duty. In one scene, James stands dumbfounded in the cereal aisle at a supermarket after returning from combat in Iraq, experiencing frustration and a sense of disappointment, perhaps because his decisions appear now to be inconsequential and his civilian existence mundane—in stark contrast to his gritty experiences in Iraq. Mark Boal, screenwriter and coproducer of *The Hurt Locker*, describes the scene, "The supermarket scene is one that veterans in particular have pointed out to me—it's probably the single scene that they talk about the most, which is surprising to me. It really seems to ring true to a lot of them in the sense of capturing that feeling of being lost when you come back to a normal life" (Gaita, 2010, p. 1).

In the spirit of the "performance narrative," a genre in ethnography, we employ examples from *The Hurt Locker* several times in this chapter as qualitative tools, using narrative fiction as a literary device to convey meaning (Chase, 2005; Denzin, 2005; Schwandt, 2007). Of course, such an approach is fraught with limitations, including sensationalizing examples from film, stereotyping, and misinterpretation. We caution the reader not to overgeneralize and to bear in mind that each student, veteran or nonveteran, is an individual. We hope that, because of the film's broad appeal and familiarity, this qualitative strategy is a useful vehicle for introducing the reader to the phenomenon of veterans' transitioning from military service to civilian life.

As more students with military experience enroll in college, the role of a helping professional on campus can be of special significance in assisting in this transition. Interestingly, college attendance can be a bright spot in the lives of veterans, including those with combat experience. For example, one research study's findings indicated that educational goals aided in the psychological healing of a severely wounded soldier, a former Army sergeant who lost a leg as the result of a roadside bomb attack in Iraq. His story "illustrates how pursuing higher education can provide a positive focus during a veteran's recovery and transition" (DiRamio and Spires, 2009, p. 85). This particular veteran chose to pursue a degree in the health-related professions and has indicated an interest in attending graduate school in the future.

College attendance can be a constructive and affirming element in the transition process, but how can administrators, staff, and faculty in a postsecondary setting better understand the contemporary phenomenon of the student veteran in transition? The key lies in uncovering and authentically understanding the underlying issues involved in the transition process. To that end, the approach used in this chapter draws from the rich history of literature and research on theories of adult transition.

Bridges (2004) suggests that every transition starts with an ending rather than a new beginning, which may seem counterintuitive but has useful application when trying to more deeply understand a student's journey from military to civilian life. He defines endings and identifies four Ds—disengagement, disidentification, disenchantment, and disorientation—all of which help to understand the process an individual experiences when leaving military service and entering civilian society. For example, when a soldier is discharged from duty, disengagement may be the key, and, as Bridges notes, "with disengagement, an inexorable process of change begins. Clarified, channeled, and supported, that change can lead toward . . . development and renewal" (p. 113).

In the early stages of an individual's transition from member of the armed forces to student on a college campus, some level of support should be provided by the higher education institution to increase the probability of his or her academic and personal success. Bridges also describes the need for a "neutral zone" between endings and beginnings, perhaps a period of adjustment lasting six months after discharge from the military before starting college. Campus personnel will discover that some student veterans do not allow for a neutral adjustment period and rush right into school after discharge, something that should be considered when working with this student population.

For the helping professional on campus, understanding how a student's roles, relationships, routines, and assumptions have changed as the result of his or her military experiences is vital. Wapner (1981) introduces the notion of conceptualizing the impact of change using a "psychological distance map" (p. 225), where the degree to which transition alters one's daily life can be gauged. Wapner uses this technique to examine an individual's affective involvement with others in the interpersonal environment. For example, a student who has lost all contact with his former colleagues in the military will experience transition differently from someone who maintains contact.

Another critical component for understanding transition is the context, the primary setting, in which transition occurs (Schlossberg, 2007). Often, transitions are very personal and affect only the individual and a select few who are close to that individual. In another scene from *The Hurt Locker*, Sergeant James shares with his wife a disturbing story from his experiences in Iraq. His story does not go over well, and an awkward moment arises. James realizes that his wife really does not want to hear about his experiences related to the calamities of war. This scene illustrates the difficulties of adjustment, even with support from family members. In one study, a veteran remarked,

"It's kind of hard because your family can't understand, and that's the worst part" (DiRamio, Ackerman, and Mitchell, 2008, pp. 86–87).

The context for transition from military service to college involves not only the individual and close family members and friends but also the campus community—faculty, staff, and students. Students with military experience refer to context when they speak of "veteran-friendly campuses . . . where programs and people were in place to assist with transitions between college and the military" (Ackerman, DiRamio, and Garza Mitchell, 2009, p. 10).

Identifying the type of transition is as important as recognizing context when developing a clearer understanding of the individual's journey. Goodman, Schlossberg, and Anderson (2006) categorize transitions into three types: anticipated, unanticipated, and nonevent. Attending college after discharge from the military is mostly an anticipated transition and is approached in a straightforward manner. The subtleties of the other two types, however, also play a role in the lives of student veterans. One example is the financial crises that students often report soon after they start attending college, when veterans' educational benefits are sometimes slow to be processed and delayed by bureaucracy and red tape. "Oh, it's horrible, I sent my paperwork in a year ago and I'm not even sure if it's coming in yet, to tell you the truth. I checked a month ago and it still wasn't in," remarked a student (DiRamio, Ackerman, and Mitchell, 2008, p. 91). Such scenarios should be considered unanticipated transitions.

Transitions that a person expects but do not happen are labeled "nonevents." Consider the case of the returning student veteran who expects assistance with getting started in college and finds little or no support on campus. A disgruntled Army veteran describes a nonevent in that same study: "There is nothing here [at this university] for veterans. . . . I got no help. When I walked into the office it was empty and I was told I would have to make an appointment. Which was kind of weird because all the [staff] were sitting around drinking coffee" (p. 90).

The American Council on Education study, *From Soldier to Student* (Cook and Kim, 2009), reveals some interesting facts about the services colleges and universities provided for students with military experience. For example, 57 percent of the 723 institutions surveyed indicate that they provide services and programs expressly for student veterans but with "great diversity in how institutions serve veterans, the variety of services and programs offered, and where services/programs are housed within the administrative infrastructure" (p. viii). For example, only about half (49 percent) of the colleges and universities, both public and private, surveyed provide a dedicated office for student veterans, which is, as the report states, "an indication of institutional commitment" (p. ix). Regardless of institutional approach, the information presented here should be useful for considering providing services and programs for students who have served in the armed forces. (See "Institutional Response to an Emerging Population of Veterans" for more details about the Cook and Kim study.)

A helpful "equation" to keep in mind when conceptualizing transitions is shown below. Inspired by the social psychologist Kurt Lewin (1936) and his equation $B = f(P,E)$, where B (behavior) is a function of the interaction between the person (P) and his or her environment (E), ours for veterans in transition is:

$$\text{Transition}_{(individual)} = f(\text{Type, Context, Impact})$$

Here, the transition can be viewed as the function, or interaction, of the type of transition (anticipated, unanticipated, or nonevent), the context in which the transition occurs (personal versus in the community), and the impact of how the transition alters the individual's daily routines. This conceptual formula (Type, Context, Impact) should be useful as a mnemonic for higher education professionals to remember when they strive to assist students with military experience. Keep this in mind as we move forward to discuss and apply one of the main theories of transition, Schlossberg's "4S model" (1981, 1984).

A Model for Supporting Student Veterans' Transition

The experience of transition—whether changing jobs, attending college, or being discharged from the military—has several dimensions for consideration by both the person experiencing the transition and the helping professional who supports that person's journey (Schlossberg, 1981). This approach suggests a process exists that, if understood, can be managed. What is the process, and are models available as guides for understanding the phenomenon?

Schlossberg's widely studied and used 4S model details four major factors that influence an individual's ability to cope with transition and, ultimately, succeed and flourish. The 4Ss—situation, self, support, and strategies—are grounded in the notion that people bring a mixture of strengths (resources) and challenges (deficits) to each transition. Ultimately, establishing whether a person has the resources necessary to cope with a transition leads to developing supports and strategies for success. According to Schlossberg (2004), "Transitions alter our lives—our roles, relationships, routines, and assumptions. . . . It is not the transition per se that is critical, but how much it changes one's roles, relationships, routines, and assumptions. The bigger the change, the greater the potential impact and the longer it may take to incorporate the transition and move on" (pp. 3–4).

Figure 1 is an adaptation of the 4S model. This variation was designed specifically for use by college administrators, staff, and faculty to better understand the population of students who have served or are serving in the military. In this adaptation, coping with transition is portrayed as a course of action. Note, however, that the linearity and directionality implied in Figure 1 is not always applicable and that each individual's transition path is unique. This course typically involves step-by-step investigation and change, requiring an individual to work through events (often with the assistance of a helping professional) and adjust several areas of his or her life journey. For example, as detailed in the first block in Figure 1, careful consideration must be given to assessing the situation at hand. Three situational elements appear to be particularly germane to the transition of students from the military to college: control, role change, and concurrent stress.

Most transitions involve a changing of roles, which could include role loss (for example, moving out of the role of combat soldier) or role gain commensurate with attending college. Perhaps with assistance from a campus helping professional, a student can acknowledge these roles, whether gain or loss, and mitigate some of the stress associated with them. Because roles are often dictated by the expectations of others, including family, other students, and society as a whole, they are "normative prescriptions for behavior" (Zaleznik and Jardim, 1967, p. 210) and can be a source of frustration for students in transition. For example, college-level study skills, a critical component in a

FIGURE 1
Adaptation of the 4S Model

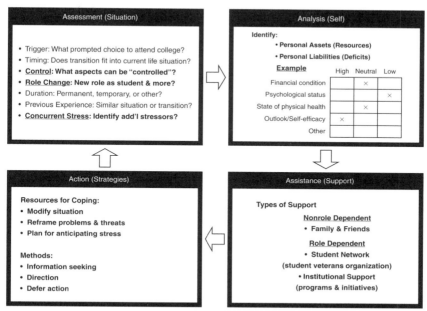

Source: Adapted from Schlossberg (1981, 1984) for use by college personnel when assisting students with military experience

student's role, can suffer while serving in the military. As one veteran in a previous study noted, "It's kind of like I forgot how I studied. Prior to leaving, I had a 3.4 GPA, and when I got back, it just went down" (Ackerman, DiRamio, and Mitchell, 2009, p. 10). Turner (1990) refers to both "cultural credibility of the potential new role pattern" and "success in gaining institutional support for the new pattern" (p. 107) among several factors leading to success in a new role. With adequate support structures in place at a college or university, Turner's criteria for transition and role change can be met.

From a pragmatic perspective based on interests and abilities as they relate to career goals, several transition assessment tools exist, many of which are available at colleges and universities. For example, Aviator is an assessment and planning software program based on the same system that the U.S. Department of Labor uses to analyze jobs (Valpar International Corporation, 2011).

Veterans in Higher Education

The use of a formal transition assessment survey, whether career or other focus, as an ice breaker between the student veteran and the college professional can be an important first step for uncovering and understanding the full range of transition issues that he or she faces.

Evaluating role change is one of the elements of a careful assessment of a transition scenario; another is characterized as control. Essentially, the source of the transition from military service to college is an internal role change choice by the student and, thus, controlled by him or her. Perhaps because of the generous education benefits of the new GI bill or pressure from other sources, however, some students do not appear to have a conscious sense that college attendance is indeed a personal choice, not to be taken lightly or hastily. This control, or lack of it, of one's own choices can be applied to Bridges's "neutral zone" mentioned earlier, in which a veteran does not take the time necessary to adjust before attending college.

The helping professional on campus can be supportive by pointing out this element of personal choice, thus providing a starting point for the student to take ownership of his or her decision to pursue postsecondary education and laying the groundwork for coping with the military-to-college transition by establishing options, particularly in the case where the student rushed immediately to school after being discharged from the armed forces. Some delay for adjustment might be advisable. In fact, although it is common for people to associate the post-9/11 GI bill directly with a college education, these same Department of Veterans Affairs educational benefits may also be used under certain circumstances for apprenticeship and on-the-job training programs (U.S. Department of Veterans Affairs, 2008).

Many situations where transitions are required are likely to be stressful to some degree. When combined with concurrent stressors such as attempting to reunite with loved ones after a prolonged absence during military service or dealing with emotional or health difficulties as a result of combat duty, the possibility of being overwhelmed during transition periods increases, often substantially. Being able to identify these stressors and plan for mitigating their intensity is something that a higher education professional, including faculty, can help with, particularly to provide a referral for where to seek additional help. After a thorough appraisal of the transition scenario and identification of stressors, perhaps with the assistance of a helping professional, a shift in focus to a self-analysis of the transitioning individual is the next step.

Once again it is important to note that much of the theory behind the 4S model hinges on the idea that individuals bring both strengths and liabilities to the transition process. They are resources and deficits. The example in Figure 1 uses a simple rating scheme for evaluating the characteristics that are likely to be relevant for coping with change. The example given is oversimplified and is intended to provide the reader with a starting point for conducting or helping a student perform a self-analysis pertaining to coping with transition. The personal characteristics to be considered may include an individual's status pertaining to socioeconomic standing, whether he or she is a first-generation college student, gender (research on women with military experience is an emerging subtopic in the literature on student veterans), age, ethnicity, psychological and health condition, and personal characteristics related to self-efficacy, spirituality, values, and resiliency. The process of self-analysis itself can be of immense help to an individual in planning for a successful transition. Keep in mind that some veterans may have unrealistic expectations based on their experiences with recruiters, the Department of Defense's transition program (known as "TAP"), and Veterans Administration counselors. Moreover, the ability to spot and attempt to correct the liabilities that stand in the way of a positive transition from military service to college attendance will likely prove invaluable. Where can assistance be found to lessen the effects of personal shortcomings and deficits?

As indicated in Figure 1, assistance and support can be found in both non-role dependent and role-dependent environments. Non-role dependent support typically comes from family and friends, people who view the transitioning individual as a loved one, not as a soldier or a student. This type of support may be essential for a successful transition, but is likely outside the scope of influence of the helping professional located on campus. Support based on a role such as that of a student in a collegiate setting is provided in the form of student organizations, campus programs, and other institutional initiatives. The influence of a student veteran organization on campus can be powerful in establishing social connections between students with similar interests and experiences. As noted by Summerlot, Green, and Parker (2009), student veteran organizations "serve as an important starting point for student veterans who are new to a campus, helping them to find information about support services and opportunities" (p. 75). It is a role-dependent form of assistance because typically only matriculating students in good academic standing are encouraged to join student organizations. What about others who choose not to get involved in a student organization? What support can they seek?

Institutional assistance is integral to aid students in transition, and a holistic approach to that assistance is preferred. According to Cook and Kim (2009), a majority of colleges and universities are considering providing professional development for faculty and staff for dealing with the issues facing many student veterans and exploring external both public and private funding sources to finance campus programs for veterans. More than half of the institutions surveyed indicated a commitment to increase the counseling services available and improve referral procedures for off-campus counseling.

Findings from research on adult learners in general indicates that these nontraditional students, of which students with military experience are a subpopulation, prefer multiple modes of instruction to accomplish their educational goals (Caffarella, 2002; Knowles, Holton, and Swanson, 2005; Merriam, Caffarella, and Baumgartner, 2007). Choosing which school to attend "is influenced by institutions' abilities to offer a variety of delivery modes and flexible scheduling" (Cook and Kim, 2009, p. 7). Thus, not surprisingly, nearly 90 percent of institutions with services for student veterans report offering alternative formats for curricula delivery (Cook and Kim, 2009).

Referring again to Figure 1 and the actions required once support is identified, it is important to recognize that transition strategies are likely different for each individual and are based on the results from the previous steps of assessment, analysis, and assistance. Considering, however, that a Rand study estimated that nearly one in three veterans has PTSD (Tanielian and Jaycox, 2008), it is possible that psychological counseling may be warranted. For example, counseling can help a student develop strategies for reframing problems and threats (Hackney and Cormier, 2005). Information-seeking behavior such as finding tutoring to improve academic performance and to sharpen study skills should be encouraged. In general, the actions and strategies of the transition process are cyclical and, as noted by Goodman, Schlossberg, and

Anderson (2006), "perhaps one of the most important interventions we can apply to help a person establish or reestablish hope" (p. 113).

Conclusion

In another scene from *The Hurt Locker* (2008), Sergeant James speaks to his toddler son about how much his life has changed since serving in combat in Iraq: "You love playing with all your stuffed animals. You love your Mommy, your Daddy. You love your pajamas. You love everything, don't ya? Yea. But you know what, buddy? As you get older . . . some of the things you love might not seem so special anymore. Like your Jack-in-a-Box. Maybe you'll realize it's just a piece of tin and a stuffed animal. And the older you get, the fewer things you really love. And by the time you get to my age, maybe it's only one or two things. With me, I think it's one." James's monologue to his son reveals an important point to consider. He describes how, as we grow older, the number of things we love diminishes, perhaps even, as he says, down to one. Sadly, an addictive compulsion for the intensity and thrill of war is James's most persistent and apparently sole passion in the movie. As the film concludes, we find out that he has volunteered for another combat tour in Iraq. Although *The Hurt Locker* is a fictional work, albeit based on real experiences, one wonders whether in real life such passion in an individual can be redirected to postsecondary educational pursuits contingent on seeking assistance in the transition process.

The implication for helping professionals in higher education is that a student veteran's postsecondary educational journey and the pursuit of a college degree can be a positive force in his or her transition. Research on transition, however, indicates that these students will need support. "Supporting the troops" is not simply a cliché, a slogan, or a bumper sticker. It requires a caring individual, perhaps a helping professional on a college campus, to make a concerted effort to assist in the transition process, perhaps using the 4S framework presented in this chapter. These students are neither overly needy nor disgruntled; they simply need assistance in getting started, and once set on a positive path or trajectory for success, their maturity, discipline, and initiative will lead them to personal accomplishment and academic achievement.

Commentary from Nancy K. Schlossberg
Student Veterans and Transition

Nancy K. Schlossberg spent most of her career as a professor of counseling psychology. She taught at Howard University, Wayne State University, and twenty-six years at the University of Maryland, College Park, and served as president of the National Career Development Association. Schlossberg is the author of nine books. She is copresident of TransitionWorks, a consulting firm, and professor emerita at the College of Education, University of Maryland, College Park.

Dr. Schlossberg: Veterans deal with multiple transitions. They are leaving the military, along with their colleagues. Even though there is relief, even excitement about returning home, they are leaving the familiar, their friends, and sense of mission. At the same time that they are dealing with "role exit" matters, they are moving into two new systems: reintegrating with their families and starting college. We love to picture the male or female soldier coming home to a warm, loving family and getting back right into the groove, but that's not reality. We are really discussing a series of complex and complicated transitions.

Student services and counseling services are key to establishing transition programs that could make a difference. It would be useful to identify and visit model programs in the country for clues that could be modified for local programming. The following suggestions might serve as a starting point:

Step 1. *Set up a one-to-one support system* so that every veteran has an individual with whom to explore expectations and feelings. Establishing these "socializing agents" can be the cornerstones of a successful transition. The first consideration is to understand the challenge of moving into any new system, which requires "learning the ropes." There is a great deal of confusion about any new system. Certainly, going to college for the first time is an enormous challenge, especially for veterans, many of whom are unable to clear their minds so that they can focus on the textbook they're supposed to be reading or the paper they're supposed to be writing.

Step 2. *Establish a group situation with weekly meetings.* I wrote (1981; Goodman, Schlossberg, and Anderson 2006) about the work of Robert Weiss (1975, 1976) and how he dealt with helping people in transition after a divorce. Of course, that's a different transition, but his model can be adapted for veterans. Whenever I've set up a transition program for populations new to me, I conduct focus groups as a way to ensure that the participants define their major concerns. Nobody else can walk in their shoes, but it is important to listen and be responsive to their voices.

The group meetings would pair the new veterans coming to college with veterans who have successfully negotiated the transition. An experienced group leader could steer the discussion so that it dealt with an underlying issue: the confusion, the ambivalence, the thoughts that you can't control, etc. Many of these veterans felt that they were doing something important, that they mattered to their country, and performed beyond what most people can do. Now, they have come to college and are often treated like children. There are many things that potentially could make them feel put down. Here they are, men and women, strong in the military and now they are children in the classroom.

Step 3. *Establish group meetings with veterans' significant others.* The veterans are trying to balance school and family. Often family members might not understand what is going on, and they too need to share their feelings. For example, assume a soldier is in a family with two or three children and that that returning veteran is expected to help at home; meanwhile, he or she has a paper due. It's about balancing; it's the same old, same old-balancing work, family, and school.

This topic is very important. If we can ease the way through intentional student service programs, we too would be making a contribution to our country. It takes a lot of guts to start school, but education will be their stepping stone to a better life.

What Matters to Veterans? Peer Influences and the Campus Environment

TRANSITIONING FROM MILITARY LIFE TO CIVILIAN LIFE is difficult enough, but trying to fit in on a college campus is "a culture shock that's hard to adjust to," said Michael Dakduk, the deputy executive director of Student Veterans of America (J. Johnson, 2010, p. 1).

The Military Bond

An evening seldom goes by that we do not hear on the nightly news about young soldiers from the war zones of Afghanistan and Iraq. When interviewed, the young men and women speak movingly about the bonds forged as they work together to accomplish their common goal. Upon returning to civilian life and for many, a college campus, the interdependency and cohesiveness created and nurtured in the military unit remains key for student veterans. As one recently returned student veteran put it, "As a member of a military unit, individuals are taught to work as a team to achieve a mission and once an individual gets to the college level they struggle when everything is in their hands only" (Auburn University Veterans Task Force, 2010, p. 11).

Knowing how important the concepts of team and connectedness are for this population of students, what can higher education personnel do to leverage this idea and better understand the needs of returning student veterans? Ample knowledge exists about the importance of peer groups in the nonveteran college population (Antonio, 2004; Astin, 1993b; Dey, 1997; Milem, 1994, 1998), but significant gaps exist when applying that knowledge to student veterans. This issue is important for veterans. Junger (2011) characterized the phenomenon:

Brotherhood has nothing to do with feelings; it has to do with how you define your relationship to others. It has to do with the rather profound decision to put the welfare of the group above your personal welfare. In such a system, feelings are meaningless. In such a system, who you are entirely depends on your willingness to surrender who you are. Once you've experienced the psychological comfort of belonging to such a group, it's apparently very hard to give up [p. 276].

As one student who served in Iraq and suffered a life-changing injury noted, "I thought I'm so motivated, so intelligent—I am taking on the school. It didn't happen that way at all. I was so lost" (Alvarez, 2008, p. 1). The title of this chapter refers to Astin's classic *What Matters in College?* (1993b). The purpose here is to explore and integrate existing knowledge about peer groups in the campus environment with the information we have about student veterans.

Inputs, Environment, and Outcomes

It is helpful when looking at the effects of peer support for student veterans in the college environment to frame this view through multiple lenses, beginning with the overarching themes from Astin's framework of inputs, environment, and outcomes (I-E-O). Inputs refer to factors and characteristics affecting students at the time of college entry, the environment comprises the experiences the student has in the college environment, and outcomes are characteristics the student demonstrates after exposure to the environment. Growth is assessed by comparing the student at the beginning of college with the student at the end and identifying what factors in the environment might have contributed to this change (Astin, 1993b). Astin's I-E-O is a framework for research rather than a theory per se, and it is how I-E-O is used here: to frame an examination of students who have military experience and their college journey.

Inputs
Underlying the I-E-O conceptual framework is Sanford's early work (1966) in student development research, which outlines the concept of the developmental conditions of readiness, challenge, and support and how these conditions

affect behavior. Applying this relationship between person and environment, we find, like with all students, a variety of readiness factors that affect veterans as they enter college. Among these factors are demographic variables and academic preparation. Demographic variables include military status, gender, race, age, marital status, socioeconomic status (SES), disability, and sexual orientation. For example, and despite popular belief, students with military experience are less likely to be married at the age of 22 than are their civilian counterparts, 10 percent versus 13.6 percent, respectively (U.S. Department of Defense, 2009a), and service members are more likely to have earned a high school diploma, 92.5 percent versus 82.8 percent, respectively (U.S. Department of Defense, 2009b). Thus, consideration should be given to the idea that Astin's "input variables" can indeed have an impact on student veterans and are not just for application when considering traditional-age college students. In addition, factors relating to psychosocial readiness, necessary for veterans as they transition from the military and assume their newly independent status as a college student, can further complicate their chances for success.

Environment

Environmental factors that exert a strong influence on veterans are the quality and quantity of peer relationships they developed in the military. How to uncover and experience a similar kind of camaraderie for the student veteran in the college environment presents a challenge in this essential component in the college transition. From Astin's work, we know empirically that "the student's peer group is the single most potent source of influence on growth and development during the undergraduate years" (Astin, 1993b, p. 398), so an assumption could be entertained that the peer groups with which the student veteran identifies and affiliates might provide the support necessary for his or her success in college.

The environmental supports provided by university programs, policies, and people are critical variables in the equation of success for students with military experience. For example, administrators at a community college in the state of Washington received federal grant funding to create a computer code for their existing student notification progress system to identify veterans who experience academic difficulties (U.S. Department of Education,

2010a). Other initiatives that are emerging at campuses across the nation provide peer support through organized veterans' groups, learning communities, and various student organizations (Ackerman, DiRamio, and Garza Mitchell, 2009). Student organizations formed by veterans are gaining in popularity. In 2007 only a handful of campus-based student veterans organizations existed; that number has grown to more than three hundred nationwide (Sismour, 2010). Encouraging involvement in other areas of campus life such as student employment, counseling, tutoring and transfer, and returning adult students' programs not only helps student veterans but also offers global insights for nonveterans. The worldview and humanity veterans bring to the campus are vastly different from those of young Millennials, who depend on parental authority and whose need for approval may not extend far beyond acceptance in his or her organization of choice. For some older student veterans, additional campus challenges may lie in the apparent immaturity observed in typical nonveteran peers and their extended adolescent journey. One student, a junior majoring in business administration, who had served two tours in Iraq, described the challenge of the differences in maturity levels by noting "it's difficult dealing with college age kids. The things they care about, like parties and girls, they don't feel important to me" (Gasendo, 2008, p. 1).

Outcomes

Empirical evidence supports the notion that strong identification with a peer group, particularly out-of-class interactions that reinforce in-class concepts, can bolster academic success and that interactions with peers may be as influential, perhaps critically so in some cases, as the experiences in a college classroom (Astin, 1993b; Pascarella and Terenzini, 2005). Additional research clarified the role of peer groups on the development of college students and identified conditions that affect the influence of peer groups (Milem, 1998; Newcomb and Wilson, 1966). The conditions are size of the group, homogeneity of the group, isolation of the group, and influence of group attitudes on individuals. Military culture places strong emphasis on the group—the combat unit, for example—and, in that context, the fundamental nature of peer bonding is found in social relationships based on teamwork and trust (Siebold, 2007). Feldman and Newcomb (1969) identified peer groups as "membership" groups with agreed-upon norms that develop through interpersonal interaction (Antonio, 2004), and research findings support the notion that personal interaction among members influences individual behavior (Astin, 1993b; Chickering, 1969; Dey, 1997; Milem, 1998). The literature also reflects the idea that the peer group and a student's individual development are directly influenced by the "values, beliefs and aspirations" of the peer group (Astin, 1993b, p. 398).

Inputs, Environment, and Outcomes for Veterans

Astin's I-E-O framework provides a starting point for conceptualizing the psychological and sociological setting that a traditional-aged student population would likely encounter in college, but it is also useful for understanding students who have military experience. He describes the peer element as "a collection of individuals with whom the individual identifies and affiliates and from whom the individual seeks acceptance or approval" (Astin, 1993b, p. 400). We suggest that this definition is also a good fit for the group of returning student veterans and have labeled this adapted framework, I-E-O-v. The "v" in the adaptation of Astin's framework, representing veterans, is exemplified by the comments of this student who served as a helicopter mechanic and crew chief in the Army, "We knew we needed a group for soldiers to get together for peer support and to make it easier to adjust to school life and civilian life" (Zoschke, 2010, p. 1). As this definition is applied to the student with military experience, one question to consider is whether the psychological constructs of identification and affiliation have different meanings for veteran and nonveteran students.

Because we know that much of what is learned in college occurs outside the classroom and is tied to the social aspect of learning, how does this knowledge apply to student veterans and individual connections to peers in and out of the classroom? In their 2008 article, DiRamio, Ackerman, and Mitchell identify this peer connection as a transitional, social survival process used by student veterans to "blending in." Without the opportunity to engage with peers in and out of the classroom, one veteran identified this blending in as remaining anonymous in class. As this veteran put it, "I don't actually like to stand out too much" (DiRamio, Ackerman, and Mitchell, 2008, p. 88). Another young man blended in to connect to peers outside the classroom by joining a fraternity: "I embraced [Greek life] simply because I didn't have anybody up here at the time" (p. 88).

Providing opportunities for student veterans to interact with peers in the classroom and to use peer-supported study groups outside the classroom will go far toward alleviating this feeling of isolation. Adapting Maslow's Hierarchy of Needs (1954) in Figure 2 to a student veteran framework presents interesting parallels among the basic needs of food, shelter, and safety. These survival needs have been met and reinforced in the military environment through camaraderie and peer support, where literally a soldier's survival depends on peers and the bonds forged on and off the battlefield. Many veterans, particularly those in the National Guard whose units have been dispersed upon leaving combat, struggle with the loss of belonging to a group, some so much that they desire to return to the battlefield in an attempt to maintain the connection (Holmstedt, 2009). The lack of real connectedness in the college environment for student veterans may be tantamount to having safety and physiological needs such as financial stability and good health unmet, leading to feeling isolated and disconnected and needing to just blend in. Because many veterans of war have experienced a Hobbesian world where laws and rules were unreliable, they may have a different definition of Maslow's safety needs. Their idea of safety may be one where comrades in arms rely on each other to gain military advantage and achieve some semblance of security (Henderson, 2002).

Social and academic integration in the new environment leads to persistence not only in attaining academic goals but also in achieving intellectual and social competence that contributes to a sense of purpose and self-awareness. The attainment of belonging and affiliation that was an essential part of being in the military contributed to satisfying the need for achievement and self-esteem. For the student veteran to persist and move into the role of a fulfilled civilian self, he or she must experience this belonging and connectedness in the college environment.

FIGURE 2
Adaptation of the Hierarchy of Needs for Student Veterans

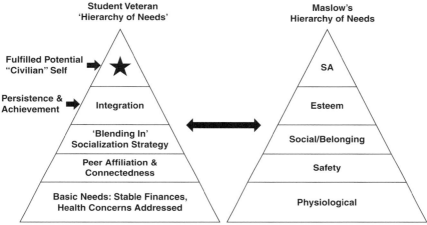

Source: Maslow, 1954.

Peer Group Supports and Influences

The development of personal identity is a task of young adulthood (Chickering, 1969), and for many student veterans, this identity is solidified in the military environment and may be challenged in the campus environment, where identity is more loosely defined. What impact does being a veteran on campus have on relationships with peers? Does veteran status make it difficult to identify and affiliate with nonveteran peers? Does the Shakespearean phrase "band of brothers," popularized in the book by historian Stephen Ambrose (1992) and the Emmy award–winning television miniseries that aired in 2001, and its application to identity for veterans and the bonds forged in a wartime scenario provide for automatic affiliation and inclusion with other veterans on campus? One student veteran organization at a small private college in Nevada has as part of its mission statement a welcome to "our band of brothers and sisters. As a group, we will give those who have joined a feeling of energy, support, knowledge, and excitement to face tomorrow's challenges" (Veteran Student Alliance at Sierra College, 2010, p. 1).

For some the need to be identified and acknowledged as having served in the military is key, while others may choose to re-create or establish a nonveteran identity by concealing their veteran status (Rumann and Hamrick, 2010). Identity is based on a belief structure about personal values and self-regard (Chickering and Reisser, 1993; Kegan, 1994), and these beliefs affect the peer group with which one connects. The significance and impact of the peer group are directly influenced by the frequency and intensity of the interaction with the group (Astin, 1993b; Milem, 1998), while the group's norms, beliefs, and behaviors provide the framework around which members approve of and accept each other.

In the military, these structures are well established and rigidly applied. If expected behaviors are not adhered to, then removal from the group is immediate; there is no room for deviation from the group norms. Hierarchy and homogeneity in the military peer network are time honored and respected. This teamwork and affiliation are essential keys to physical and emotional survival in the military. The frequency and intensity of those connections, which contribute to the magnitude of the peer group effect (Astin, 1993b) have been well documented historically as well as in the arts and literature. In *The Hurt Locker,* for example, the norms and experiences of the group culture of war far outweighed the desperate need of the lead character to reenter civilian life. Allegiance to one's own combat unit can be a most powerful force, as noted by a service member who opted to go back to the war zone because "his fellow soldiers depend on him" and "there is nobody else in the unit doing my job, I don't have a choice" (Stone, 2009, p. 1).

So, given the strength of the unspoken bond among veterans, does this connection provide for automatic identification and acceptance in the veterans' group? What about affiliations with nonveterans' groups? How does this "environmental fit" affect the persistence and integration into the campus? Tinto's Model of Institutional Departure (1993) outlines the attributes necessary for social and academic integration (see the following chapter), which include preentry characteristics, goals, and institutional experiences. According to this model, the key to persistence lies in the student's perception of the connections and the significance of peer interactions in relation to the veteran's adjustment needs. A student who was a lieutenant colonel in the Army and served in Iraq assumed a leadership position in a veterans initiative on campus to "hook veterans up with one another in a social network," as "some veterans . . . are socially awkward and this helps" (Alvarez, 2008, p. 1).

If the college years provide a psychosocial moratorium (Erikson, 1968) where students try on various roles as they grapple with adult identity, then how does this fact relate to young veterans who have established a military identity, including combat duty, which is separate from the identity necessary to thrive in the classroom and on campus? The development of a student civilian identity as one dimension of self is critical for veterans as they make a successful transition to the college environment (see "Crisis of Identity?").

In addition to a search for identity, another task in young adulthood is the struggle with intimacy versus isolation (Erikson, 1968). If veterans have adopted this combat identity and the emotional insulation necessary in a wartime environment, how does it get played out in the social atmosphere of college? Is the typical struggle for intimacy experienced by many young people even greater for student veterans?

When asked how service in Afghanistan had changed him, a veteran expressed "shutting off feelings" and "not seeing the world as bright anymore" (*New York Times,* 2010). Another student veteran remarked, "Apparently, I've got this mean, scowling look all the time where I frighten certain people away. Which is something I'm working on, mainly because, you know, I want to get a date" (DiRamio, Ackerman, and Mitchell, 2008, p. 92). These expressions of sadness and anger affect peer relationships, which in turn may contribute to a sense of isolation and lack of connection that some student veterans may experience.

Summary and Recommendations

The application of both the I-E-O (Astin, 1993b) and the student veteran I-E-O-v models offers insights into a student veteran's postsecondary pursuits. Identity and affiliation contribute to a significant extent toward their social footprint and psychological well-being. Like other subpopulations in college, student veteran status serves as an overarching microenvironment (Antonio, 2004), which may be further subdivided into mini or micro groups based on race, gender, disability, age, and sexual orientation. Other input variables include the demographic markers of readiness such as preentry characteristics of academic preparation, first-generation status, and socioeconomic status.

The Veterans Upward Bound (VUB) program was designed to address concerns about the preentry characteristics of college-bound veterans (U.S. Department of Education, 2010b). The VUB program is part of a group of initiatives known as the TRiO programs funded by the U.S. Department of Education that offer free college-preparation assistance and cater to low-income, first-generation student veterans. Preparedness to learn is an issue here, especially when considering that many of these students may also suffer from cognitive impairment as the result of exposure to a concussive blast from an improvised explosive device. A junior studying international business described his difficulties: "My mind was blurred, cloudy all the time, and I was walking around in a daze. I had a full load and I dropped all my classes except two. And yet I'm studying all the time. It was so frustrating. [Over time] I just started to remember better, adjusting how I think. It's still very hard. With classes like regression analysis, I'll never be the same again" (Alvarez, 2008, p. 1).

The initial variable in the I-E-O-v framework, "input," is profoundly affected by a peer-dominated military environment before the student enters the collegiate environment. The socialization process that the student veteran experiences insists that he or she balance and adapt to the norms associated with college. It is where the application of multiple identities (Jones and McEwen, 2000) and a student veteran's ability to identify with and navigate within peer subgroups can be helpful (see "Crisis of Identity?"). This situation poses a central issue that takes into account the psychological and sociological aspects raised by Astin: What effect does the particular college environment that the student veteran enters have on how the student will develop? If the veteran's peer group provides automatic acceptance and approval, how impactful is the greater environment on the veteran's academic and social success? Do the interactions with nonveteran peers contribute to the environmental effects for the student veteran in ways similar to those for the typical student? These questions should be considered in future research on this emerging student population. Other traditional inputs such as age, gender, race, and level of prior education all factor in to the input variable and may be confounded by the combat experiences the student brings. If the student veteran enters a campus environment with a sizable veterans' population that demonstrates similar group values, this peer group will exert a strong influence on the cognitive and affective outcomes the student experiences.

The importance of peer connections among student veterans is supported by national organizations such as the Student Veterans of America (SVA). This group, founded in January 2008 by a University of Michigan–Ann Arbor student, is a coalition of campus groups from across the United States designed to provide peer-to-peer networks for veterans who are attending college (Student Veterans of America, 2010). The SVA was cited as being instrumental in helping achieve the passage of the Post-9/11 Veterans Educational Assistance Act, the new GI Bill that was signed into law on June 30, 2008. According to the president of the SVA, "Veterans on campuses bond because they have shared experiences that have created a brotherhood, a family so unique to their lives. . . . We have the ability to advocate for the needs of student veterans and change the future for [them] forever" (Mostafavi, 2011, p. 1).

The concept of peer group effects is well documented in the higher education literature (Astin, 1993b; Pascarella and Terenzini, 2005). Although the application of these effects has not been specifically studied as they relate to the population of student veterans, it is helpful to analyze their impact on the development process as student veterans engage with peers in the college environment. A question arises as to what extent being a student veteran influences peer effects such as attitudes about diversity. One interpretation of how the demographic of race may affect student veterans is through identification and affiliation with a racially diverse peer group of veterans and nonveterans that provides acceptance, approval, and support in the larger and perhaps more challenging environment. Given the diverse racial and cultural interactions that student veterans have experienced before college, are student veterans subject to some of the same racial segregation observed in their nonveteran college peers? Or are the effects of gender, race, and socioeconomic status different in this population because of prior exposure? Does socioeconomic status regarding enlisted versus officer matter when the veteran becomes a student? Again, these and other questions that may arise from this discussion encourage future research with student veterans on a college campus.

The transition from a team-oriented, peer-dependent military environment to a college campus where the "frog pond effect" (Antonio, 2004; Pascarella and Terenzini, 1991) invites comparisons to nonveterans from both academic and social perspectives may present challenges for the newly returning student veteran. The concept of blending in as a social strategy provides a minimal buffer for a short period but is not enough to support the persistence necessary to attain a fulfilled civilian self. Finding a niche on a large campus through peer connections, returning adult programs, and learning communities designed for veterans can provide the support and structure necessary to assist in this transition.

Commentary from Alexander W. Astin
Student Veterans in College

Alexander W. Astin is a leading authority in the field of higher education. He is professor emeritus of higher education at the University of California, Los Angeles, and founding director of the Higher Education Research Institute at UCLA. He has served as director of research for both the American Council on Education and the National Merit Scholarship Corporation. He is the founding director of the Cooperative Institutional Research Program, an ongoing national study of some 12 million students, 300,000 faculty and staff, and 1,600 higher education institutions. Astin has authored twenty books and some three hundred other publications in the field of higher education; he has received awards for outstanding research from more than a dozen national associations and professional societies.

1. Dr. Astin, what are your general thoughts about student veterans who are attending college after returning from military service?
We should be able to learn something from experience with the original GI bill, although the conditions today are very different from those days. It's always an easy cop-out to say that we need to do more research, but in this case I really believe that we should. And it should be funded by the Defense Department; that's the least they can do for men and women who have performed under extremely difficult circumstances. Because many of today's young veterans are not from college-educated families, we should also take a look at what we have learned from research on the "first-generation" college student.

2. How do you see your work and research as applied to college students with military experience?

Unfortunately most of my and others' research on undergraduates has looked at traditional-age students, so we must be careful in applying that knowledge to the older veteran. One of the most critical issues is the type of college the veteran attends. I expect that the "disconnect" that the newly entering veteran might experience upon starting college would be much less in a public commuter institution than in a residential liberal arts college.

3. Do you have any recommendations for practitioners who will be working with this emerging population of students?

The most important thing is to avoid stereotyping such students. Aside from their age and the fact that many are first-generation college students and many are married, I'm not sure that it's possible to generalize much about this group. Treat each as an individual with unique needs, aspirations, and talents.

I'm pretty sure that the involvement principle works with just about every student, including veterans. To succeed, they must become involved, and the secret to working effectively with such students is to determine what forms of involvement work best and to encourage the student along these lines. This could mean developing good study habits, becoming involved in particular campus activities, finding friends to study with, choosing a living situation (private apartment, on campus, etc.) that facilitates academic involvement, finding on-campus employment, etc.

Transition 2.0: Using Tinto's Model to Understand Student Veterans' Persistence

RECOMMENDATIONS BASED ON FINDINGS from research studies on student veterans suggest that connecting with peers—that is, other students who have military experience—is an important initial phase of the collegiate journey and a key component of later academic success (Allen and Haynie, 2008; DiRamio, Ackerman, and Mitchell, 2008; Holloway, 2009; Rumann and Hamrick, 2010). Peer connections are only a first step, however. What happens after a student makes the peer connection, perhaps by taking an orientation class with other transitioning veterans or joining the student veterans organization on campus? What are the chances he or she will persist in college? The Veterans Administration reports that veterans are using an average of seventeen out of thirty-six months of their Post-9/11 educational benefits and that only 6 percent had used the entire thirty-six months (Field, 2008). The implication is that these students are not completing four-year degrees. Moreover, frequently cited literature about student departure, including research by Tinto (1993, 2000) and others (Berger and Milem, 1999; Braxton, Hirschy, and McClendon, 2004; Pascarella and Chapman, 1983), cautions that if a student only comfortably connects with like-minded peers and those with similar experiences and backgrounds (whether civilian or military), it is more likely that he or she may depart from school before graduation. Why would a student leave college, and what are the implications for today's emerging population of students returning from military service?

Consider that the number of veterans who were continuing or starting their studies in fall 2009 was approximately 460,000 and was expected to grow as much as 30 percent per year, depending on the operational requirements of the military (U.S. Department of Veterans Affairs, 2009a). At that growth rate, by fall 2013 nearly 5 percent of total college enrollment in the United States will be students with military experience, with a majority having served during the periods of conflict in Iraq and Afghanistan. This population of students is distinctive in many ways and like other underrepresented groups in American higher education is worth studying in terms of persistence and degree attainment.

Tinto's longitudinal model of student departures (1993) provided a conceptual framework for this chapter, with the model adapted for use in considering the case of a college student with a military background. It is important to note that Tinto's model, while popular and cited regularly, is not without its critics, including Braxton, Sullivan, and Johnson (1997), who supplied empirical evidence of its shortcomings. In general, the criticisms of Tinto's model include that it is applicable only for studying traditional-age students, that it is insufficient in modeling student attrition, and that academic integration is not an important predictor of attrition (Metz, 2004–2005). Nevertheless, the adapted model presented here is useful for an introductory discussion of student veterans' persistence and academic success. A graphical representation of the adaptation of Tinto's model is presented in Figure 3.

Transition and Preentry Attributes

Research studies have identified important factors related to a transitioning service member's journey into civilian life and college (Ackerman, DiRamio, and Garza Mitchell, 2009; Bauman, 2009; Livingston, 2009). These factors manifest themselves in the form of what Tinto called "attributes," which are personal characteristics of a student that are present when he or she first considers attending college. Several of these attributes are common to all students, whether or not they have military experience. They include the attributes presented in Tinto's research, which focused mainly on traditional-age students who attended college directly from secondary school. These common attributes such as family background, socioeconomic status, prior schooling, and skills and abilities all affect a student's initial intentions before entering college

FIGURE 3

Adaptation of Tinto's Longitudinal Model of Institutional Departure for Student Veterans

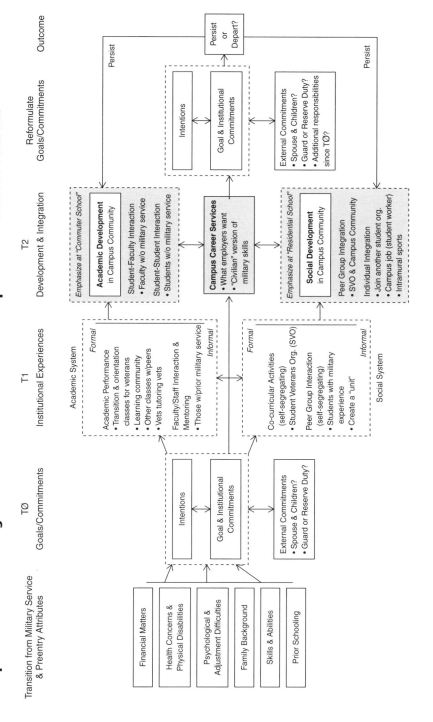

and point to the veracity of the commitment to persist as well as shape the student's goals. Figure 4 lists some of the most common preentry attributes and factors as well as goals and commitments to be considered when studying student veterans' persistence or departure.

"Tø" in Figure 4 denotes "time zero" or the period just before a student actually attends college. Among the preentry factors, research findings list financial concerns as a top obstacle in transition (DiRamio, Ackerman, and Mitchell, 2008). Bureaucratic red tape in the process of receiving educational and other benefits, coupled with the general expenses associated with starting a new "civilian" life, can present a heavy financial burden for the college-bound veteran. Often, the stark reality for transitioning veterans is that they no longer receive direct military assistance in housing, childcare, and transportation. A student may now receive educational benefits under the post-9/11 GI bill, but it is quite different from the type of comprehensive support he or she may have been used to when on active duty. And although the latest educational benefits are considered generous when compared with previous legislation, they still may not cover many of the monthly expenses and contingencies that an adult in today's society faces, particularly for a full-time student with spouse and dependents. Tinto's assertion that these sorts of issues can affect a student's initial postsecondary goals and commitments is evident here. How can college administrators and key personnel assist this emerging student population? It starts with an awareness of the preentry attributes and conceiving of ways to help mitigate some of the difficulties faced by student veterans who are transitioning from military duty to college. Failure to do so will increase the chances that a student will depart the institution without graduating.

Students who have military experience have additional attributes to consider, particularly individuals who have experienced repeated deployments and have served in combat zones. A surprising number of today's veterans have physical or psychological injuries. For example, more than 30 percent of veterans of the Iraq and Afghanistan wars sought treatment at Department of Veterans Affairs (VA) health care facilities nationwide during 2002 to 2008, and 50,000 of them were diagnosed with PTSD (Seal and others, 2009). A Rand study estimated that 31 percent of veterans overall have PTSD (Tanielian and Jaycox, 2008). Veterans who suffer from PTSD can get help

FIGURE 4
Attributes, Goals, and Commitments of a Student Veteran Before Attending College

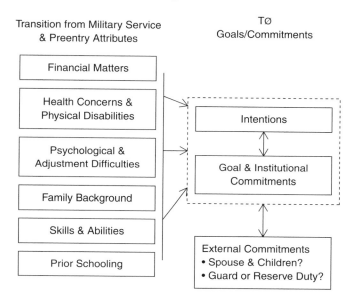

through referrals to qualified counseling or treatment through the VA health care system, which has dedicated increased resources to the treatment of psychological trauma (Rosenheck and Fontana, 2007). It is a serious matter for college administrators to consider, because the treatment of PTSD is very specific and likely outside the purview of a college or university counseling clinic where short-term treatment is the focus *(Science Daily,* 2010). Therefore, it is vital that the student, his or her family, and a helping professional address these issues before attending college. If untreated or unaddressed, students who suffer from physical or psychological disabilities will likely begin their postsecondary pursuits at a disadvantage that will negatively affect persistence and degree attainment.

Although the military is generally regarded as a representative cross section of American society, it is no secret that many men and women join the armed forces to escape bleak employment prospects and economic hardship. For these individuals, military service is a way up and out of difficult economic circumstances. One study that focused on college student veterans indicates that many indeed do join the armed forces with the explicit intent of earning money for college (DiRamio, Ackerman, and Mitchell, 2008). For example, in that study a "female participant, a single mother, noted, 'That was my motivation [to enlist]: education, I suppose, and a better life for my daughter.' The majority of women in this study joined the military for primarily economic reasons" (DiRamio, Ackerman, and Mitchell, 2008, p. 81). Therefore, it is important for college personnel to acknowledge that it is likely that many of the students who attend college after military service may have come from families with lower socioeconomic status and could be first-generation students.

Evidence suggests that students with military experience are more mature than their civilian counterparts. Moreover, these veterans have acquired skills and abilities through their military service—skills often connected with a college core curriculum—such as being globally aware and culturally adept. These preentry attributes, possessing fundamental skills and abilities, will have an effect—presumably positive—on the intentions, goals, and commitments that affect a student's dedication to persist. Tinto included this factor in his model, and the implication for student veterans is described in the next section. A word of caution is necessary, however: these students may actually become discouraged if their armed forces experience and transcripts (often from military training and prior civilian schooling) are not evaluated in good faith, whether accepted for credit or not, at the college or university. Problems associated with evaluation of academic transcripts and assessment of military experience have been identified in the literature as barriers to a successful transition (Burnett and Segoria, 2009). Moreover, diminished academic skills, especially in mathematics and study skills, brought on by years of military service and a significant gap in time since high school or previous college attendance were commonly reported among veterans (DiRamio, Ackerman, and Mitchell, 2008).

Goals and Commitments

Tinto (1993) noted that "individual commitments take two major forms, goal and institutional" (p. 43). He defined goal commitment as a student's dedication to his or her own occupational goals and the resolve to achieve the educational objectives required to reach those goals. The notion that these students, as a result of their maturity and military experience, will likely come to college with specific job-related goals is important and will be addressed later in the chapter and in the adapted model. For example, a recently discharged service member with a goal commitment to be a schoolteacher, thus continuing in public service (which is not unusual for former military personnel), will have a commensurate commitment to the educational goals required to achieve teaching licensure. Obviously, the strength of a goal commitment significantly affects a student's persistence in college. The other component of time zero, shown in Figure 4, is institutional commitment, which symbolizes the student's loyalty to the college or university that he or she chooses to attend. Family tradition (allegiance to one's alma mater) and perception of the quality of the education to be received are two factors that can affect institutional commitment. Similarly, as in goal commitment, institutional commitment plays a part in how strong the student's resolve is to persist at the institution. External commitments play an important role in the "departure puzzle," which Braxton (2000) describes as the phenomenon in American higher education where more than 25 percent of students who enter four-year institutions and 50 percent of those who enter two-year schools depart at the end of their first year. It is important to consider that the student who is older and has delayed college until after serving in the military is more likely to be married and have parenting duties as well as obligations to continue serving in the National Guard or reserves. Clearly, these external forces affect goals and commitments, thus further complicating the chances for premature departure from college. Depending on campus resources, college personnel can help alleviate the impact of these external commitments by offering programs and services for the families of students as well as assisting those who continue to serve part time in the military (T. Johnson, 2009).

Initial Institutional Experiences

The idea of helping students with military experience to meet each other on campus, thus facilitating the formation of strong peer ties and meaningful relationships, is a worthwhile initial strategy for transition and adjustment. These types of peer connections for student veterans are consistent with Tinto's model and are characterized in Figure 5 as "T1" or time one institutional experiences and activities. Tinto posited in his model that interactive institutional experiences at an academic level, between the individual and other students as well as between the individual and faculty members, "are seen to enhance the likelihood that the individual will persist within the institution until degree completion" (1993, p. 116). With student veterans, research indicates that initial interaction with other students who have military experience and with faculty members who are veterans is desirable (DiRamio and Spires, 2009). Moreover, college administrators can work to create opportunities for these sorts of interactions. For example, these opportunities, which occur within what Tinto referred to as the "academic system" (see Figure 5), can range from a formal initiative such as creating an orientation class designed for and taken exclusively by veterans who are transitioning from military service to college to an informal situation like connecting a student with a faculty member who is also a veteran and could serve as a mentor.

Figure 5 shows "T1" interactions in what Tinto referred to as the institutional "social system"; they play an important role in persistence as well. For example, joining the student veterans organization is an excellent way for some students to connect with their veteran peers in an environment outside the classroom (Summerlot, Green, and Parker, 2009). Moreover, creating less formal but nonetheless important social relationships with other students who have similar experiences is a natural way for a student to feel more comfortable at the institution. These students may form a "unit," much like that found in military culture, with this group dynamic serving as a catalyst for navigating initial institutional experiences, both in and out of the classroom. It is important to note, however, that all of these activities, both the academic and social examples presented here, are "segregating" strategies that are appropriate for the initial T1 experience but fail to help the student veteran fully transition and integrate with the broader "civilian" campus community. Research on student persistence indicates that if a student fails to ingrate both academically and socially with the broader campus community, he or she is more likely to depart the institution (Braxton and Lien, 2000; Tinto, 1993, 1997). For that matter, is a student veteran's transition really completed at the point

FIGURE 5
Initial Institutional Experiences and Activities Associated with Student Veterans' Persistence

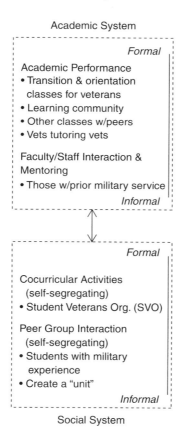

T1
Institutional Experiences

Academic System

Formal

Academic Performance
• Transition & orientation
  classes for veterans
• Learning community
• Other classes w/peers
• Vets tutoring vets

Faculty/Staff Interaction &
Mentoring
• Those w/prior military service

Informal

Formal

Cocurricular Activities
(self-segregating)
• Student Veterans Org. (SVO)

Peer Group Interaction
(self-segregating)
• Students with military
  experience
• Create a "unit"

Informal

Social System

where he or she has self-segregated into a cohort of fellow veterans, or should a successful transition include further academic and social integration with the broader campus community? What are the implications for persistence if he or she fails to do so?

Transition 2.0: Academic and Social Integration

Tinto's assertion that at some point a student should begin to deemphasize the self-segregating, peer-only behavior and start emphasizing integration with the broader academic and social community present on campus is noteworthy when exploring the phenomenon of the transitioning student veteran. He notes that "some degree of social and intellectual integration and therefore membership in academic and social communities must exist as a condition for continued persistence" (1993, p. 120). Interestingly, this idea of student development and transition has broader implications than persistence only, which is why Figure 6, a critical component adapted from Tinto's model, shows the college's career services unit as playing an important role in integration and development, particularly in the area of preparation for civilian employment.

It turns out, however, that employers, many of whom prefer to hire veterans because they appreciate the skills, abilities, and attributes veterans gain from military duty, covet a "civilian" version of the desirable skills and abilities that individuals with military experience possess. In fact, 50 percent of the 429 hiring professionals in one survey reported making specific efforts to hire veterans, but 60 percent in the same study indicated that many veterans have difficulty adapting to the workplace culture (Society of Human Resource Management, 2010). Undoubtedly some of the student veterans attending college today need to learn to adapt themselves to a civilian corporate culture, which is often markedly different from military culture, particularly during a time of war. Gary Profit, senior director of military programs for Wal-Mart and a retired brigadier general, stated that it is "the responsibility of the job seeker to figure out if they [sic] will fit well into the company's culture" (Overman and Leonard, 2010, p. 1). One way that college administrators, especially those in the career counseling field, can assist students with military experience to acquire the requisite skills for employment is to create opportunities for "civilian" academic and social development in the broader campus community. Interestingly, according to Tinto (1975, 1993) and others (Braxton, 2000; Braxton and Mundy, 2001–2002), doing so will also increase the likelihood of students' persistence and degree completion. Making the important step from self-segregated peer support to the development of a civilian version

FIGURE 6
Social Development and Academic Integration of Students with Military Experience

T2
Development & Integration

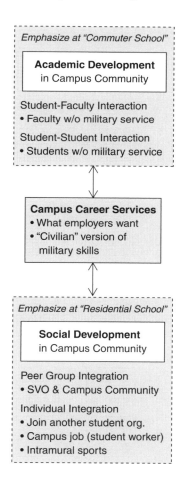

of skills necessary for career success through exposure and interaction with faculty and students from across the campus is the essence of the concept of Transition 2.0, which also signals a furthering of a comprehensive transition from military service to civilian life.

Transition 2.0: Academic and Social Integration with the Campus Community

How can a student who has self-segregated with his or her fellow veterans move toward integrating with the broader campus community? One answer may be found in what Tinto referred to as "marginality versus centrality." "In some respects, the experience of adult students is not unlike that of minority students. They too can feel marginal to the mainstream of institutional life" (Tinto, 1993, p. 76). The idea here is for students to have exposure to a variety of intellectual concepts and erudite ideas, many of which may be unfamiliar in the military setting, so they can continue to develop cognitively and begin making meaning of their experiences, transition, and the "civilian" world in which they now find themselves. This learning can be accomplished through meaningful interaction with faculty members and students who do not have a military background. It may, however, also require an intentional effort by campus personnel, in both academic and student affairs, to make consequential academic integration possible through innovative campus programs and services. One thing to consider is that, in their empirical study of Tinto's model and propositions, Braxton, Sullivan, and Johnson (1997) found a plausible link between lack of academic integration and student departure in a commuter school. One application of that finding in this context is that, at a commuter college or university, an emphasis on academic integration for student veterans, and not social integration, would be the best use of resources to increase persistence. Therefore, a campus administrator at a commuter school should look for programmatic opportunities for student veterans and faculty members, for example, to interact in a dynamic setting, perhaps in sponsored colloquia, where thought-provoking and issue-oriented ideas are discussed and debated. Of course, it is difficult to predict what the outcome might be from a heated discourse about volatile issues such as foreign policy and global conflict, but these sorts of opportunities have traditionally been a hallmark of student interaction with the broader campus community (Rhodes, 2001). Moreover, the wide variety of ideas and concepts that a student veteran is exposed to in college through academic integration will positively affect his or her career after graduation, especially in terms of the diversity of skills needed to succeed in the workplace.

Social integration with the broader campus community is also important (Braxton and McClendon, 2001–2002). Stepping out of a peer-supported faction consisting exclusively of like-minded students who have military backgrounds and moving toward social integration with the broader community can ironically first be attempted through the peer group itself. For example, the student veterans organization, as one of many student organizations on campus, can partner with other student groups, perhaps in support of a mutual cause like fundraising for a charitable purpose. In this way students will necessarily mingle in a social environment, and relationships with others outside the student veterans organization may emerge. Again, student affairs personnel could look for opportunities to support this type of interaction between student groups. An individual student veteran, however, could also integrate socially by joining another student organization, taking a campus job, or playing intramural sports. Note that strong empirical support was found linking social integration, subsequent institutional commitment, and persistence at residential universities but not in commuter settings (Braxton, Sullivan, and Johnson, 1997).

Career Services and the Student Veteran

We noted previously that a significant number of employers actually prefer to hire veterans and have initiatives to do so but that they want the job candidate to possess a civilian version of military skills and qualities. This area is where personnel from the career services unit on campus can play a vital role for students who are transitioning from military service to college. Findings from one study in which counselors from a college career services unit conducted interviews with student veterans revealed that indeed job preparation and culture shock were among the major career development concerns (Armstrong and Pruett, 2009). Moreover, recommendations from that same study included creating career classes for student veterans in which they learn about themselves while developing personal and professional goals as well as learning about the work world and how to make career-related decisions. This example shows how the career counseling unit can assist students with military experience to make the transition from the armed forces to college and ultimately career. Initiatives of this sort led by the career services unit on campus could make a significant difference in the transition of student veterans by exposing them to the needs of the civilian workforce and improving their chances of persisting at the institution through development and integration.

In "Job Outlook 2010," employers ranked three "Transition 2.0" proficiencies out of the top six most important skills and qualities for job candidates to possess (National Association of Colleges and Employers, 2010): communication skills, interpersonal skills (relating well with others), and teamwork skills (working well with others). Many students will have acquired these types of skills in the military, but skills should be further honed through academic and social integration, particularly with the assistance of career services personnel and others on campus.

New Goals and Intent to Persist

After some measure of academic integration and social development with the broader campus community and a clearer understanding of occupational goals through support from career counseling have occurred, students will, according to Tinto, frequently reevaluate their goal commitment and institutional commitment. He notes that "such experiences continually act upon individuals' evaluation of their educational and occupational goals and their commitment both to the attainment of those goals and to the institution" (1993, p. 120). Figure 7 depicts the longitudinal view of this reformulation activity and the subsequent decision to persist, that is, to continue with academic and social development or depart the institution.

Critics of Academic and Social Integration

Some have argued that a push for academic and social integration is inappropriate to impose on students, particularly student populations like racial and ethnic minority groups (Biggs, Torres, and Washington, 1998; Rendón, Jalomo, and Nora, 2000). The idea is that integration is assimilation in a pejorative

FIGURE 7
Reformulation of Goals and Commitments Based on T1 and T2 Experiences

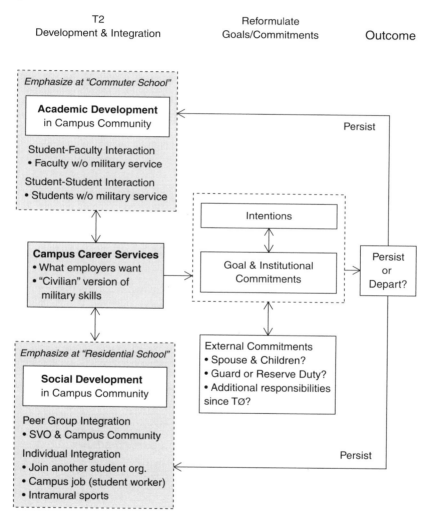

sense, and thus the implementation of that type of student development strategy in a college setting interferes with a student's discovering his or her own racial or ethnic identity. Concerns of inappropriateness for application with student veterans may arise, because it appears that, on the surface, academic and social integration is actually proselytizing a liberal epistemology, which it is not. But the notion of Transition 2.0 is not asking a student veteran to abandon any of the closely held principles and beliefs that he or she acquired while in the armed forces. Moreover, the ideas presented here for improving transition and increasing persistence are not normative in nature and are neither ideologically liberal nor conservative. On the contrary, the focus here is on acquiring a civilian version of the skills necessary to succeed in the workplace as well as increasing the chances of the student's persisting and attaining a degree, all under the auspices of academic integration and social development with the broader campus community.

Conclusion

The ideas presented in this chapter are mostly theoretical, with little or no empirical evidence existing at this time to support the claims. This adaptation of Tinto's longitudinal model of student departure for use with student veterans, however, provides a starting point and a framework for future research. Each part of the adapted model provides ideas for variables for further study. Moreover, some practical applications for college personnel to consider have been presented, including programmatic ideas for both academic and student affairs administrators. Because students who have served in the military are essentially adult learners and thus possess strong occupational goal commitments, this framework presents a win-win scenario, first in the form of opportunities for academic and social integration in college and a chance to acquire and practice the skills necessary to succeed in the civilian workforce and, second, in increased chances for a successful transition from military duty to civilian life, persistence at the institution, and completion of their collegiate journey to graduation.

Commentary from John M. Braxton
Student Veterans and Persistence

John M. Braxton is professor of education in the department of Leadership, Policy, and Organizations at Vanderbilt University. His research interests center on the college student experience, the sociology of the academic profession, and academic course-level processes. He has published more than 80 articles in refereed journals, books, and book chapters.

Dr. Braxton: Veterans would be attending college after returning from military services, but my main concern is what the institutional destination would be. I think residential colleges and universities might be problematic. The reason is that so many residential colleges and universities have student populations that are primarily the traditional college age, from seventeen to twenty-two or so. Many of them don't have older adults attending classes. There might be some residential colleges where that would be the case and those institutions where they have a proportion of older students might be a good place for them to attend, but I think highly residential and very traditional-age student bodies would be a problem because they wouldn't be able to fit in so well in the residence halls, and they might have difficulty making friends and things like that.

Another point is that veterans might find the student culture of being an undergraduate as unproductive, given that they may have more sharply defined career goals and so forth that might get in the way. I think that commuter schools might be a better match simply because of the lack of residence halls and because the social communities are not so well formed—or in many cases not formed at all. Students just come and go; they may happen to make connections with other students in class through a study group or project, with social interactions springing up around that. Also, commuting colleges and universities have a lot of students who are married, have children, are divorced with children, and are working while going to college. This makes for a different basis for their experience in going to college, one that might be more along the lines of what a veteran might be seeking—namely, an affiliation with taking courses and meeting degree requirements.

Community colleges could be an excellent entry point because their academic skills are a bit problematic and those institutions very frequently offer remedial or developmental courses. Again, veterans' experiences are going to

(Continued)

primarily be defined by their course taking, and academic support must be in place, especially the kind that you'd find at community colleges. Also, having courses at flexible times is a good idea, because some student veterans may be working. We don't know what kind of financial resources they're going to have, which is something that needs to be addressed.

Getting jobs for them on campus rather that off campus is important, as the research shows (Astin, 1984; Beeson and Wessel, 2002; Pascarella and Terenzini, 2005), and on-campus employment will go a long way toward making the student veteran more a part of the institution. In the book I coauthored with Amy Hirschy and Shederick McClendon (2004), we described an upper limit to how successful retention rates can be at a commuter school; that idea should be considered when investing resources toward veterans' academic success. I would think that online courses would be valuable to these students. I also think that much of the responsibility resides with faculty members to provide teaching techniques that will complement the learning needs of veterans and others at commuter schools. It seems to me that faculty who intentionally engage veterans in the classroom, in the learning process, and through the course materials will contribute to their persistence.

Crisis of Identity? Veteran, Civilian, Student

IN THE MILITARY ENVIRONMENT, the expectation is that individual identity becomes secondary to the identity of the group. One young man noted that "his real mission in life—in the Army—is being there for his troops" (Lewis and others, 2005, p. 368). The aggressive, male-dominated ethos, the rituals of wearing the uniform, the pride in belonging, all contribute to the collective identity. To thrive in the military, one must develop a "goodness of fit" and accommodate group norms. The sociologist Toennies (1957) called it *Gemeinschaft,* which refers to a culture in which belonging is pervasive. Winslow (1998) described the cultural phenomenon this way: "Individuals exhibit strong allegiance to their group and the group exerts social control over the individual member. In the military, group allegiance is seen to be essential to combat effectiveness. Strong affective ties bind soldiers into a fighting unit in which they are willing to sacrifice their lives for each other. Military culture emphasizes 'belonging.' . . . *Gemeinschaft* is perceived as a positive state in the military" (p. 345).

When the term of service has ended and the veteran begins to move on, the paradigm of *Gemeinschaft* likely persists in his or her consciousness. One veteran, a junior in college who spent eight months serving in the Middle East as a translator, described it this way: "It's part of your identity. It's something you carry around with you" (Arora, 2008, p. 1). Josselson, renowned for her work on identity development (1996), conceptualizes the notion of identity: "Identity links the past, the present and the social world into a narrative that makes sense. It embodies both change and continuity" (p. 29).

So how does this "change and continuity" affect college students with military experience? Does the military identity, while still present and an integral part of "self," at some point recede and become overlaid with a postveteran civilian identity, which in the college environment incorporates a newly acquired status as student? How does prior knowledge of self translate during the transition from veteran to student? What role does an understanding of metacognitive awareness of other's reactions to self and relationships to others play in solidifying this new student veteran identity? What challenges does "straddling" multiple roles bring to the student veteran? What are the implications of identity development for students with military experience, and how can college personnel, including administrators, staff, and faculty, assist this emerging student population? These and other questions are addressed in this chapter as we discuss the framework for identity development in student veterans.

Identity Development and Knowledge of Self

The developmental path that incorporates a sense of identity is most closely tied to the work of Erikson (1968) and is defined as a psychosocial process that combines cognitive growth and environmental challenges. Chickering's framework (1969) for identity as the pivotal vector in his explanation of how students develop grew out of Erikson's theory of identity development as an evolving sense of self that changes and adapts (or maladapts) when one encounters challenges in the environment. This definition is highly salient for college student veterans, for during the transition from active duty to student, which for many may be during their young adult years, their previously determined identity is bombarded by differing relationships and external factors they may confront in a new environment. The need to reformulate an identity arises out of a state of disequilibrium and discomfort resulting from the conflicts between what established identity dictates and what changes are being faced. These changes may come from outside pressures, cultural norms and expectations, and personal life events.

In Kegan's theory of self (1994), how people understand and make meaning of the world around them determines and influences their identity, self-concept, and interpersonal relationships (Lewis and others, 2005). According to King (2009), the cognitive domain must take the lead in how a person makes meaning of the world. Underlying a growth in cognitive development is the concept of "perspective taking" (Kegan, 1994; Lewis and others, 2005), which frames a sense of self. For most college-age students, this move toward "self authorship" (Kegan, 1994; Baxter Magolda, 1992) is not accomplished until they are more advanced in college. On the return to the college environment, the student veteran who has developed a strong prior knowledge of self faces additional challenges to the military identity he or she may have established. The shift to student status for some will prove more difficult and will depend on a number of situational and support factors in the new environment.

Self and Others

This cognitive growth parallels Perry's model (1968) of increasing levels of ambiguity in how students think and relate to the world. The younger student's thinking is more dualistic and based on absolutes; as he or she progresses, thinking takes on a less concrete worldview. As students mature cognitively, they are able to entertain others' ideas and grapple with issues from multiple perspectives. The ability to reflect on how behavior affects others and to think about thinking provides the basis for identity formation, moral decision making, and relationships with others. This domain may provide a greater challenge for the veteran in the college environment during the period of transition. Although the academy has rules, it also has flexibility and questions regarding adherence to rules are encouraged. To apply Perry's positions (1968), the military environment demands a good measure of dualistic thinking, while one goal of higher education is to adopt relativism.

In the study by Lewis and others of identity development in early-career West Point cadets (2005, p. 369), traditional-age military students understood and expressed ideas about their world based more on concrete rewards and self-interest than mutuality. Developmental changes in their thinking did occur as they got older, but the internalization necessary for mature introspective decision making was not evident in the first years of the military program.

Not surprisingly, in Chickering's framework (1969), the development of integrity is one of the last vectors to be achieved and is closely tied to the emergence of a true identity. This domain is aligned with the growth in cognitive development and the knowledge of a sense of purpose. Experiences in this domain may be limited for some student veterans, as purpose and decision making have been defined by the reliance on external authority found in a military environment. Navigating in an environment where finding a purpose is an individual task can be a struggle and requires an awareness and acceptance of independent and interdependent thinking.

The ability to interact with others who are different and not be threatened by their difference is an important part of a fully integrated identity. A certain level of metacognitive awareness is necessary to enable one to gauge responses to self and to others that requires the perspective taking discussed by Lewis and his coauthors (2005). For the student veteran, a number of relationships have been predetermined in a strict hierarchical environment, and the transition to a less programmed civilian world can present a challenge. In the military, decision making involved following the rules that were supported by outside forces. In the college environment, self-regulation is key to a successful transition. The personal relationships the veteran has developed may or may not be sustained outside the military environment, and prior civilian relationships will be affected by factors in the veteran's established identity. How these challenges are met and the environmental supports provided contribute to successful balance as the veteran makes the transition.

Multiple Roles and Intersecting Identities

Although a number of students may be challenged by adapting to the college environment, particularly if they function in additional roles such as parent, worker, and caregiver, the status of student veteran adds yet another layer to the complexity of intersecting identities. In addition to the social identities of race, culture, sexual orientation, and gender, other preentry variables such as first-generation status, officer or enlisted rank, socioeconomic status, and disability all differentially affect the veteran as he or she enters the academy. In the familiar world of the military, the social and personal context for what constitutes a visible and acceptable identity is narrow; the "dominant values dictate norms and expectations" (Torres, Jones, and Renn, 2009, p. 577). As explained by Abes, Jones, and McEwen (2007), the multidimensional filters that were effective in one context may need to be reframed and adjusted as the student veteran faces multiple intersecting domains in the college environment. When different cognitive, interpersonal, and intrapersonal influences are encountered in college, the student veteran's identity shifts and reforms to create a multidimensional model that incorporates various features into the proportionality of the "goodness of fit" for the student veteran in the "new" environment of college. How the veteran adapts and copes with these changes can be determined by the level of transition experienced; the timing, support, strategies, and sense of self that were in place before the transition (Schlossberg, 1984); and the commitment made to the development of a new core identity.

Schlossberg, Lynch, and Chickering (1989) provide a useful starting point for considering the transition of students with military experience. The Moving In, Moving Through, Moving Out model is used to study the dynamics of transition and to identify factors that individuals must cope with to succeed. When moving in and out of the phases of this model, a person evaluates each transition over time while reflecting on the likely positive or negative effects as well as considers the resources available to him or her for use in managing change. This process is not easy; as one student who spent thirty-four months in Iraq and Kuwait remarked, "I was more scared of college than I was of the Marine Corps, and that's the truth" (Tillo, 2011, p. 1).

Part of the self-analysis recommended by Schlossberg and her colleagues includes conducting an inventory of strengths and weaknesses based on personal traits, psychological factors, and social supports available. Thus, coping strategies are formulated for the individual to use in modifying the situation, controlling the meaning of the transition, and managing stressors (Schlossberg, Lynch, and Chickering, 1989). It is during the Moving Through college phase that a crisis of identity can emerge, and research confirms that such crises occur during transitions (Erikson, 1968). One former service member who experienced some measure of identity crisis described the difficulties of transitioning to college this way: "I ended my time in the Marine Corps as a platoon

FIGURE 8
Models Used to Understand the Identity Development of Students with Military Experience

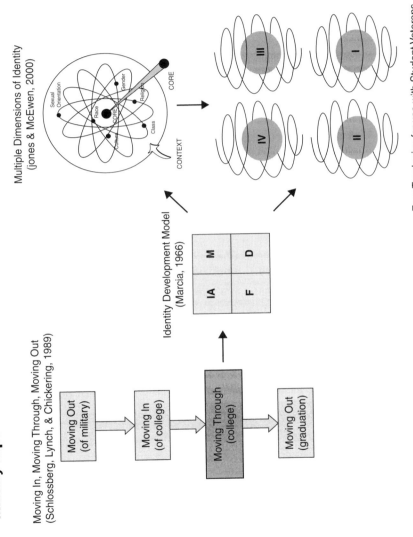

Moving In, Moving Through, Moving Out
(Schlossberg, Lynch, & Chickering, 1989)

Multiple Dimensions of Identity
(Jones & McEwen, 2000)

Identity Development Model
(Marcia, 1966)

Four Typologies for use with Student Veterans

sergeant, and the way we deal with things in the Marines is different. I caught myself yelling at kids in discussion groups" (Arora, 2008, p. 1).

This chapter approaches identity development in the student veteran population through a multidimensional lens that integrates self, others, and the environment. Different from a linear model, this multidimensional view of identity is fluid and is affected by a person's response in interpersonal, intrapersonal, and cognitive domains. The models depicted in Figure 8 are the theoretical bases for understanding the complex nature of student veterans' identity.

Crisis, Exploration, and Commitment

Particularly applicable to student veterans at a time of transition, Marcia's theory of identity formation (1966) provides a vehicle to understand how young people navigate and reconcile crises. According to Marcia, the two variables in identity formation are exploration and commitment. In the exploration stage, a crisis is experienced, and information seeking either clarifies or challenges previous values. The commitment stage occurs when the values and beliefs are confirmed and then acted on. Four statuses in the exploration and commitment stages—foreclosure, moratorium, diffusion, and identity achievement—attempt to explain how the crises and commitments work together. Unlike Erikson's stages, they do not necessarily occur in a progressive pattern. We believe this framework has particular relevance and application to the student veteran during the period of transition from a military environment. They form the basis for the creation of the four typologies depicted in Figure 9, which were developed to help explain identity development in this population.

Multiple Dimensions of Identity

McEwen (1996) and Jones and McEwen (2000) describe multiple dimensions of identity as the intersections of various contextual categories that make up identity development. This conceptual model, represented as a helix-like structure, contains a core identity or self, which McEwen calls the "unified self." The knowledge of self can be likened to a type of Johari window (Luft, 1969), with personal identity somewhat protected yet open in different contexts. For

FIGURE 9
A Framework for Creating Four Typologies of Students with Military Experience

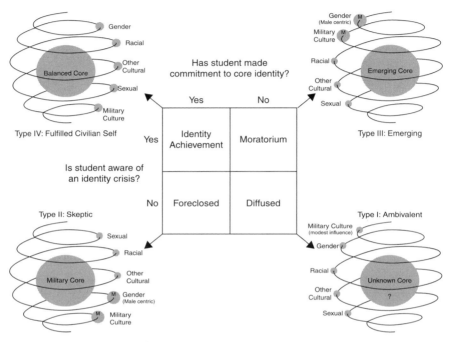

Source: Marcia, 1996; Jones and McEwen, 2000

example, when considering one dimension of identity in a military context, the status of sexual identity had been hidden by rule of law (but repealed during this writing [Dinan, 2010]) in the "don't ask, don't tell" policy (P.L. 103–160). This new law affects both the interpersonal and intrapersonal domains and therefore a sense of self, particularly for the student with military experience who is transitioning to college.

The various social dimensions of identity such as gender, race, culture, and sexual orientation exert different influences on "self" at different times, depending on their relative importance in context. This social construction of identity involves expectations of others, societal norms, and the various dimensions of identity (Torres, Jones, and Renn, 2009). In addition to the aforementioned social dimensions, we suggest that the context of first-generation status and socioeconomic status plays an important role in the identity puzzle for the student veteran and so include these parameters in our discussion. To better understand identity development of students with military experience, we introduce and discuss four typologies to help define the student veteran's path to a civilian core identity.

Typologies

Typological models highlight differences among people based on the way they think or act. Perhaps the most familiar example of the use of typologies is the Myers-Briggs Type Indicator (Myers and McCaulley, 1985), which measures psychological preferences and categorizes individuals into sixteen possible personality types. It is important to note that no normative values are associated with typological categories; one type is no better than another type. This sort of methodological neutrality is desirable when classifying college students and is preferable to demographic stereotyping using race, gender, or other categories. Typological models also provide an alternative to traditional college student development theories such as psychosocial or cognitive approaches.

The application of typologies for better understanding college students has a rich history in the higher education literature. A frequently cited and seminal work by Clark and Trow (1966) uses student attitudinal data about college attendance and involvement to create four distinct typologies. Despite generational differences and the age of their study, Clark and Trow's findings describing four classifications of dominant student groups—the academic, the collegiate, the vocational, and the nonconformist—are still relevant today, including application in this study.

Astin (1993a) used data from the Cooperative Institutional Research Program survey, a multiinstitution and longitudinal study, to describe seven student typologies. His findings yield student groups with similarities to Clark and Trow's but include new types such as "the artist" and "the status striver." Astin's findings, along with those from other typology studies (Katchadourian and Boli, 1985; Horowitz, 1987), support the idea that student types are relatively stable over time. This study adds to the literature on student typologies, with a focus on the identity development of students with military experience.

Type I: Ambivalent

These students can be characterized by a diffused sense of self. They show little commitment to their old military identity and have not adopted a new identity or see the need to change to adapt to the new environment. They sense no crisis of identity, and their former military life exerts a modest influence, with the other dimensions of identity having an impact only as issues arise. For ambivalent students, change is effected by external rather than internal pressures. When it comes to selecting a major or getting involved in social organizations (even the student veterans organization), these students lack a desire for a commitment to any of the typical occupational or ideological areas. Perhaps the ambivalence stems from a sense that people cannot or will not understand the experiences of a veteran, a scenario evident with an art student who served three deployments to Iraq. He "usually doesn't tell fellow art students about his life in the military 'because they can't relate'" (Hancock, 2007, p. 1).

This is where a helping professional in student or academic affairs can assist the ambivalent student to move toward identity exploration and the development of internal rather than external sources of authority. Unfortunately, the lack of commitment to the exploration of a new core identity that is seen in these students is more likely to put them at risk for departure and noncompletion of a degree. If they find a connection or are challenged by a crisis, then "lost–sometimes found" students, as characterized by Josselson (1987), may move into Type III: Emerging.

The ambivalent student's situation may be exacerbated by problems with mental acuity, a symptom of injury from a concussive force such as a roadside bomb explosion, or psychological difficulties, perhaps an undiagnosed case of PTSD. In one study a student veteran remarked, "Once I got back to school, it was like I know what I need to do and it is right in front of me, but I'm just not doing it. I don't know if it [is] because I am not as focused as I was before I left. . . . I don't know" (Ackerman, DiRamio, and Garza Mitchell, 2009, p. 10). College personnel should be aware of the issues that a Type I student may be facing, be prepared to make a referral or referrals for qualified help, and follow up with the student.

Type II: Skeptic

Skeptics live with a continuing commitment to a military core identity, which serves as their dominant sense of self. The other dimensions of their identity are "foreclosed," and in this state, these students experience no crisis and no need to explore other aspects of identity. The student veterans who fit this type may have achieved goals in the military by never questioning authority and continue to expect their role will be as receivers of knowledge in a culture that supports this allegiance. Although this approach may have been effective and even necessary in the male-dominated military culture, a certain amount of frustration may arise in the academic environment as the military identity is relegated to a smaller piece of the multidimensional identity puzzle. Unless a crisis is experienced in foreclosure status, no need exists to change and the commitment to the identity status quo remains static (Marcia, 1966).

The risk for skeptic veterans is how to cope when challenges arise to their established military identity. Do they move into moratorium status and emerge, or does the challenge outweigh the support (Sanford, 1969) and they leave? One student, a former Army sergeant, described her focus when she remarked, "Coming back from not only being in the military but also from war, you realize all of the advantages we have here in the United States, and so you're career-oriented and driven and you want to go through school as soon as you can to get back to a job" (Tillo, 2011, p. 1). In this example, the student does not view the collegiate experience as one where identity dimensions are to be explored but as a straightaway process where job training and vocational preparation are paramount. She is likely "foreclosed" to change at this point, viewing her military identity as a strong asset in a linear quest for a degree without detours. Unless her narrow focus is challenged, perhaps by necessity in an exigent learning environment or with the help of a caring higher education professional, she may experience frustration and depart (Tinto, 1993).

Type III: Emerging

Those in moratorium status are not yet committed to change but sense that their military identity, which has been dominant, may not serve effectively in other contexts, particularly in the college environment. One student, a four-year veteran of the Marines and a junior, may have sensed a commitment to change was necessary when he remarked, "There's a structure in the military. You know what to do. You wake up at 5:30, train, follow your set schedule for the day, go out and do your mission, and come back and do it all over again. At a university, there's no commander or structure like that" (Mangan, 2009, p. 1). Moreover, the Type III student may experience dissonance when attempting to substitute new and uncomfortable opportunities for social interaction in college for the friendship and solidarity he or she felt while in the military. One student veteran, a history major, remarked about serving in the military: "That's camaraderie. That's brotherhood. What's their [fraternity members'] idea of brotherhood? Coming back in fifteen years and reliving the fraternity college experience, the undergrad experience? Come on" (Brown, 2009, p. 1).

Having been forced to deny other social identities (for example, sexual identity as a result of "don't ask, don't tell") and push them into the background in the military, those emerging students may struggle with the crisis encountered when the voice of authority and the development of a new voice collide. As the student development literature has pointed out (for example, Evans and others, 2009), cognitive conflict forces change. Forced change on a Type III student, however, will likely require support from campus personnel, including staff and faculty members. A report by the National Survey of Student Engagement noted that "'culture shock' is the way some veterans describe their transition from military life to college life on campus. Most don't feel they fit in. And often, institutions don't make it any easier" (Chappell, 2010, p. 1). Assistance is vital at this stage as the student seeks to discover or reestablish a meaning and purpose in life apart from military service. Moreover, according to Marcia (1966), those in a moratorium status remain with this balancing act for a short time, and most move on to an achievement status where multiple identities eventually lead to a balanced core.

Type IV: Fulfilled Civilian Self

A balanced core identity defines student veterans who have achieved a fulfilled civilian self. They have experienced crisis and questioned authority, explored identity options, grappled with the idea of change, and become comfortable with the need for interdependency (Chickering and Reisser, 1993). For example, Type IV students have established and maintained relationships with other students, faculty members, and staff (Berger and Milem, 1999; Tinto, 2000). Moreover, this student has by now worked to renegotiate roles with family members and has reestablished interdependent relationships with friends (Schlossberg, Lynch, and Chickering, 1989). Assistance from a helping professional on campus could be critical for a student desiring to explore Type IV actions and behaviors.

Ultimately, the various aspects of their identity have balanced out, with the different dimensions appropriately influencing and fluctuating as the environment dictates while maintaining the core identity. Social and academic integration in college has helped these Type IV students make substantial progress toward a comprehensive transition from military service to civilian life through an "organized set of images, the sense of self, which expresses who or what [they] really are" (Widick, Parker, and Knefelkamp, 1978, p. 2). Cognitively and affectively they have found their own voice.

Conclusion

Applying theories of identity development is helpful for understanding the emerging population of students with military experience. Student veterans who have served in this most recent decade of conflict are a relatively new phenomenon on college campuses, and little empirical evidence exists to support the ideas presented in this chapter. Applying ideas about identity development in both theory and practice to this unique student population is a starting point, however, for conducting future research. The use of typologies, their limitations notwithstanding, can be one path to creating variables for study in the area of student veteran transition, personal fulfillment, and academic success.

Commentary from Linda Reisser
Student Veterans in College

Linda Reisser is dean of student development at Portland Community College. Before arriving at PCC in 1998, she served as dean of student services at Suffolk Community College on Long Island. Reisser has been a faculty member at Columbia University and Western Washington University. She coauthored the revised edition of Education and Identity (1993), with Arthur Chickering, which describes seven vectors of student development.

1. Dr. Reisser, what are your general thoughts about student veterans who are attending college after returning from military service?

My perceptions are that student veterans returning to college now are better educated and have broader experience than those returning in previous decades. There are also more female veterans than ever before, and a good number of them have experienced sexual trauma.

Also compared with previous decades, more of them have survived injuries, and there are more physical and psychological challenges (traumatic brain injuries, post-traumatic stress disorder, suicidal tendencies, addictions, etc.). A large percentage are unemployed and coping with homelessness or relationship issues.

Colleges facing tight budgets have been struggling to find space and resources to support them. Some of us have participated in workshops and training, but more is needed, especially for faculty. We are inviting local agencies to send resource people to the campuses, and they provide vital help. Luckily, many veterans are purposeful, dedicated, and focused on meeting their learning goals. Though they may be impatient with distractions and red tape, they have experience persisting through adversity.

2. How do you see your work and research as applied to college students with military experience?

In terms of the seven vectors model (Chickering and Reisser, 1993), I see four of them having special applicability:

Managing emotions: Some veterans may need assistance with impulse control and coping with negative emotions such as frustration, anger, or depression. Development along this vector includes getting in touch with and accepting the full range of feelings, including the positive ones (hope, confidence, inspiration), and learning flexible control and appropriate expression of feelings.

Moving through autonomy toward interdependence: Veterans who functioned well in a regimented environment may need to develop self-direction, persistence, and mobility. After the camaraderie of their unit, they may be tempted to disconnect from peers, hide the stress they experience, or look for a sense of belonging with fellow veterans rather than reaching out to connect with a more diverse community.

Developing purpose: Finding a new educational or career purpose may be challenging after immersion in the unit's mission. Especially in a recovering economy, it may require openness and adaptability. Development also involves strong interpersonal and family commitments and priorities, which may have been disrupted while serving abroad. Counselors can be very helpful with these issues.

Establishing identity: This dimension incorporates the others and includes movement toward a positive, stable, comfortable sense of self, with greater awareness of both "what I am good at" and "how others see me." The changes that happened during military service need to be understood and integrated, hopefully with growing self-esteem.

3. Do you have any recommendations for practitioners who will be working with this emerging population of students?

We have learned to do the following at Portland Community College:

Listen to individual needs and encourage engagement with others. Some veterans say they want to join a club; others say they don't want to be singled out or identified as a veteran. We have tried to acknowledge the skills and knowledge veterans have to offer the campus. Those who are looking for "a team and some structure," as one Iraq veteran said, are now serving in student leadership roles.

Help veterans to find each other. A state veterans officer said, "They don't want help (or don't want to admit it), but they need help. If you can create a space for them to meet, they will help each other." We have offered stress management classes and other college survival courses just for veterans, which has become another way for them to connect with each other.

Provide training and information for faculty and staff. We need to know more about the patterns and challenges facing veterans and how we can best help them overcome obstacles resulting from their military (and life) experiences. Like all students, they are here to develop intellectual and interpersonal competence, healthy relationships, more humanistic values, and meaningful lives as global citizens. Theory and research help us to be more intentional about it!

Women Warriors: Supporting Female Student Veterans

Now, when is it you was tellin' me you'd be old enough to join the army?

Next birthday.

Then you'll be off from here?

I hope.

Good for you. Good deal. But what about the boys and—?

Woodrell, 2006, p. 26

FOR REE DOLLY, THE MAIN CHARACTER in Daniel Woodrell's haunting *Winter's Bone,* the only way out of her dead-end existence is the military. Whatever she might encounter between joining up and facing combat has to be better than what she has to look forward to in her life of poverty and violence in the back woods of the Ozarks. Though a work of fiction and certainly not generalizable to all who serve in the military, this visceral need to escape to a better life through military service has served as a catalyst for many and fueled military enrollment for women (and men) time and again. Women and men join the military for a host of reasons: a duty to country, adventure, a career, gaining technical skills or a college degree, providing for their families; moreover, recent research has shown that a number of women who enlist are escaping abusive and violent home environments (Foster and Vince, 2009).

The history of women in the armed forces in many ways parallels the devaluation of women as workers in American society in general. Although women served in large numbers in World War II, they were not afforded the same benefits or opportunities as their male counterparts. After the war, in 1948, Congress passed the first law allowing women to serve in the military during peacetime (Solaro, 2006). But this advance came with restrictions. Women officers could account for no more than 10 percent of the total number of women in the armed services and could not rise above the rank of captain or lieutenant in the Navy. They also could be discharged for marrying or getting pregnant. By the post-Vietnam era, civil rights legislation had been enacted, the draft was abolished, and the military was forced to accept women into their ranks. This de facto integration resulted in resentment and women receiving less than equal treatment, thus setting the stage for abuses of power and a lack of principled enforcement (Solaro, 2006).

The face of the current military is changing. With the capture and wounding of Private Jessica Lynch and Specialist Shoshana Johnson (Pierce, 2006), the public view of women in combat situations became personal. These women were sisters, mothers, daughters. "This is what is different about this war, women are fighting it. These little wisps of things are stronger than anyone could imagine and taking on more than most Americans could ever know" (Scharnberg, 2005, cited in Pierce, 2006, p. 97). The continuation of a voluntary military, historical events, and sociocultural shifts have adjusted the information we have about women's performance in combat. The debate continues, however, and much of it centers around the traditional societal views of gender roles. It has taken about thirty years to achieve an almost full integration of women in military service, and it has not been without costs to the women (and their families) who have returned from the battlegrounds of Iraq and Afghanistan.

Over the past decade, the number of women in the military has increased steadily; currently women make up more than 14 percent of active-duty military personnel, with 17.5 percent National Guard or Reserve and 20 percent new recruits. Of the 1.8 million troops in Afghanistan and Iraq, more than 200,000 are women. It is predicted that by 2020, 10 percent of the entire veteran population will be female (Foster and Vince, 2009). This increase seems to be the result of more than just women entering and leaving the military, the overall higher survival rates in general of women in the population, and the younger age distribution of women in the military. Moreover, in addition to being younger than their male counterparts, women have achieved a higher level of education, with more than 70 percent having some college (compared with 57 percent of men). Women are also more likely to be single parents (11 percent as compared with 4 percent of men), and 40 percent of the women identify as a minority, in comparison to 32 percent of the men (Foster and Vince, 2009).

Unfortunately, with the demographic shift in the military, the incidences of sexual assault or harassment, known under the general term of *military sexual trauma* (MST), have also increased, with one in five women responding "yes" to the question of whether they had experienced sexual trauma during their military service (U.S. Department of Veterans Affairs, 2011). In a recent *Chronicle of Higher Education* report about the health concerns of eight thousand students, about eight hundred of whom were student veterans (Killough, 2009), researchers found that among female student veterans, 43.7 percent reported having been sexually assaulted, compared with 29.8 percent of nonveteran female students.

In addition to this disturbing trend, it has been documented that although women in general are more likely to suffer from PTSD at about twice the rate of men, female veterans are often not diagnosed with this combat-related disorder (Baechtold and De Sawal, 2009). In the above-referenced *Chronicle* report, the researchers also found that among female student veterans, 14.1 percent reported that they suffered from PTSD at some point, while 5.4 percent of their nonveteran peers reported suffering from it.

Although narrative and specific health-related data on female veterans exist, a gap remains in the literature on gender differences in how military women and men readjust on their return to civilian life. The first large-scale empirical study addressing this issue was recently funded by the U.S. Department of Veterans Affairs. As a joint venture between Yale University, the VA Connecticut Healthcare System, and the University of Connecticut, this collaborative effort will be the first of its kind to empirically study whether women veterans are more likely to suffer PTSD than male veterans. This premise presumes that many women may enter the military having experienced trauma and "may suffer trauma at the hands of their comrades more than male veterans" (Yale University, 2010).

Although MST and PTSD also affect men in the military, the incidences of both are considerably higher for women. This fact raises a number of questions about our thoughts in general concerning the roles of men and women in society. Does the belief in the bastion of male turf so often celebrated in the armed services contribute to the alarming statistics? Is what we believe about men and women, that women are more nurturing and men more aggressive, continuing to affect what happens to women in the military and on their return to civilian life? If women are motivated more by care than justice, then how can they also be warriors? And if so, what happens to the young women when they come marching home and into a college environment? And how best can campuses provide support while still challenging these women?

Enduring Effects of Male Turf: Gender and Assumptions

The only gender role available for men in the military is to be a man, and to behave less stereotypically "manly" opens a man up for ridicule. For women in a male-dominated environment, however, there appear to be other gender-related choices and assumptions associated with one choice or the other. In an assessment of gender on perceptions of military leadership (Looney, Robinson-Kurpius, and Lucart, 2004), the only differences noted were the more emotionally based (empathy) characteristics attributed more to women. This outcome could be the result of the limited number of women in high-ranking military leadership roles. Fewer women have progressed to the top ranks, perhaps because they have taken off time for childbearing or because they are a single parent.

In a further consideration of gender, Herbert (1998) surveyed 285 women from all branches of the armed services ranging from seventeen to forty years of age and asked participants whether they believed that the military pressures women to act masculine or feminine and whether they perceived penalties for being too much of one or the other. She found about an even split in respondents' answers: 51 percent said no, 49 percent said yes. If a woman was perceived as "too feminine" and "doesn't adopt male mannerisms, then she is 'too feminine' to be a leader" (Herbert, 1998, p. 45). If she was perceived to be too masculine, then "a woman is naturally assertive and forward [and] it is often an affront to older commanders" (p. 46). When asked whether there were penalties for being perceived as too feminine or too masculine, 66 percent said "yes." Penalties for being perceived as too feminine included ostracism or disapproval by other women, being viewed as a slut or sexually available, being viewed as incompetent, not taken seriously, and limited in career mobility. If a woman was perceived as too masculine, she was ostracized or ridiculed, limited in career mobility, and labeled a lesbian (regardless of sexual orientation) (p. 65).

It could be that these perceptions and the close scrutiny affect the attitudes of many in the military as in other traditionally male-dominated fields and possibly contribute to the high incidences of sexual harassment and trauma that a number of female veterans have experienced.

In a recent survey of female veterans, 45 percent (sixty-six of 147 surveyed) of the women reported that their needs upon returning to civilian life were no different from those of male veterans. The most difficult challenge was the transition to civilian life, followed by the need for continuing education, and the adjustment of once again being a parent (Foster and Vince, 2009). Even with these challenges, however, women continue to serve and return home, many with the outlook reflected by this veteran's comment: "Although I experienced many problems because I was female in the military, I think it is only fair to say it was probably the most interesting and exciting time in my life" (Herbert, 1998, p. 128).

Mothers and Warriors: Care and Justice

Certain demographic attributes and personal issues factor into the transition to college for all students. For veterans, additional variables play a role in this transition. Among them are age, the reason for enlisting, marital or parental status, rank achieved in the armed services, prior college experience, and number of tours of duty. In addition, for women, the incidences of MST and PTSD are higher than for men, more women are single parents, and they are more likely than men to have had some college experience (Foster and Vince, 2009).

In a recent post from *The Gainesville Sun* (Tillo, 2011), a young woman at Santa Fe College who works in the local Veterans Affairs Office reports that she joined the Army to help fund her education. It has long been a common practice for women and men to enlist to pay for education. One of those women was a wife and mother who had been accepted to medical school (Holmstedt, 2009). Unsure of how to pay for it, she applied for and received a Navy scholarship to cover the costs. As a physician who served numerous times in the battle zone, she is currently the chief naval officer in charge of Wounded Warrior programs at Walter Reed and Bethesda and counts her duty times in Iraq as some of her most rewarding experiences. She and her family have agreed that although she would not volunteer to return, she would "go back in a heartbeat if she were asked to go" (p. 306). In her current position, she continues to serve these soldiers and says that "the opportunity to take care of these troops and to complete the loop is the reason why I stay in the military" (p. 306).

At the other end of the enlistment spectrum, like the fictional character Ree Dolly in the novel *Winter's Bone*, a number of teenage women and men who enlist are escaping from their lives and attempting to find new ones in the military family. In Holmstedt's narrative (2009), the author tells the story of one such woman, an army sergeant, who enlisted as a young woman right out of high school to get away from her abusive family. Holmstedt comments that the solider "knew she had a purpose in Iraq: to protect her fellow soldiers in a way she couldn't protect her mom" (p. 11). She felt "she had a purpose on that battlefield, whereas, back home, her mission wasn't as clear" (p. 10).

Another of the women Holmstedt interviewed served as a medic, having completed Army medical training and some nursing school. She was also a single parent. On her return home, she reported that neither "she, nor her home felt important anymore" (p. 36). It was not that motherhood was not important, but her children had been safe without her and she felt less connected. As a dedicated soldier, she worried about the continued safety of her troops in Iraq and wondered whether "her replacement would keep the soldiers safe" (p. 37).

Each of these vignettes echoes the themes of care and responsibility that are raised in much of the literature on women's development. The scenarios highlight the importance of taking care of others and feeling a responsibility to transfer that ethic of care to other situations. In Gilligan's groundbreaking work on moral decision making (1982), she proposes that women tend to operate more from a perspective of care and responsibility to others, while men more commonly base moral decisions on a system of rights and justice. Like other developmental theorists, Gilligan suggests that women's thinking about moral decisions follows a progressive sequence. This sequence begins with a primary concern for self and individual survival and progresses to a realization that in respecting and valuing self, one makes decisions from a moral compass grounded in responsibility and how those decisions affect others. It appears that women, more often than men, make different decisions based on situations and a feeling of mutuality, and the connectedness that women experience serves to help define a sense of self that is rooted in interpersonal relationships and an ethic of care.

For many female veterans who become college students and juggle multiple roles, the deeply rooted sense of a responsibility for others that they adapted to a combat situation will follow them into an academic environment. This sense of teamwork and connectedness when balanced with the justice and fairness orientation adopted from the discipline of the military become important components of success in the college environment.

Into a College Environment: Developing a Voice

Like many young female veterans, one of the young women in Holmstedt's narrative (2009) was attending college when she was deployed. Upon her return from Iraq, she found herself back in a college classroom hoping to "blend in." She did not want to draw attention to herself as a veteran and preferred to discuss the war "with people who had been on the battlefield and gone through similar experiences" (Holmstedt, 2009, p. 192). She had changed and her young classmates had not. When the students in her philosophy class went on about the war and she tried to share her perspective, she felt "silenced" (p. 192); no one seemed to want to hear her side. At one point, hearing something that went directly against her beliefs and personal knowledge, she could not let it go and she erupted, lashing out like her sergeant self dressing down a private. Holmstedt goes on to report that this classroom experience left this female veteran feeling as if her experiences on the battlefield were being "invalidated" by the students and the instructor, who remained silent (p. 193).

What occurred in the classroom for this student veteran underscores the observations made by Belenky and her colleagues as they began their investigations into why women reported that they had gaps in their knowledge and often doubted their intellectual competence (Belenky, Clinchy, Goldberger, and Tarule, 1997; Goldberger, Tarule, Clinchy, and Belenky, 1996). In many situations in the classroom and in everyday life, women often feel unheard, even when they believe they have something important to say. The young veteran's comment about having her combat life invalidated offers an unfortunate glimpse into the fragile balance that exists for some women while finding a voice.

The attribution of feeling silenced that she experienced in her classroom is usually ascribed to those women who have usually never had a voice (Belenky, Clinchy, Goldberger, and Tarule, 1997). By the nature of their lives, they have learned to be passive and view authorities as having all power. They do not speak out because they have been told their words do not matter and therefore they do not matter. Although this young woman felt silenced by the situation and initially hesitant to express her views, she took a chance and risked sharing information from personal knowledge. Belenky and her colleagues describe this process in the development of one's own voice as separate knowing, which is a way of knowing that is based more on personal experiences than on what authorities say. In this perspective, a woman's thinking demonstrates critical thought but tends to rely on more impersonal procedures that establish self as separate from others. As a woman transitions to the next perspective, connected knowing, her attempt to understand the thinking of others is greater and her struggle to achieve a balance between self and others can either be supported or discouraged by the college environment. The connected mode of reasoning would want to know not only why one thinks that way but also the steps that led to that way of thinking (Belenky, Clinchy, Goldberger, and Tarule, 1997, p. 114).

Many nontraditional students express greater concerns about their ability to succeed in college than do their traditional peers. Rendón (1994) describes the need for validation for this population by providing an intentional intervention that can serve as a support and, in this context, be considered an extension of Schlossberg's concept of mattering (1989). Schlossberg discusses the concept of mattering and identifies four components: attention, the idea that one is noticed; importance, the belief that one is cared for; ego extension, the idea that someone will attend to your personal successes or failures; and dependence, the belief that one is needed. For a number of female students to feel as though their words and ideas are heard in a college classroom, they must feel that what they have to offer matters and, as an extension, that they matter. For the young veteran in the philosophy class from Holmstedt's narrative, the responses of the students and the teacher in that classroom left her feeling that her personal experiences with war were invalidated and thus that she did not matter. For many women, the cognitive process of developing a voice is interpersonal and closely tied to connecting to others. Feeling like one matters and therefore does not become marginalized, particularly for a female nontraditional or first-generation college student, is a key component of success in the academic environment.

Help Seeking: Learning to Cope

Another critical variable in achieving success in a college environment for women and men is knowing when to ask for help, and it appears that asking for help is something that women do more frequently than men. In the military, the concept of "tend and befriend" (Taylor and others, 2000) has been observed as an effective coping strategy used in long deployments by women. If women are more likely to connect to others by using an interpersonal network of support strategies such as friends, peers, and professionals, then it seems reasonable that one of their coping mechanisms would be help seeking.

By adolescence, gender differences in help-seeking behaviors have been firmly established, with women engaging in help-seeking strategies at a higher rate than men (Boldero and Fallon, 1995; Komiya, Good, and Sherrod, 2000). A number of factors contribute to this reluctance to seek help and are related to perceived gender roles: a strong belief in individualism, low interpersonal dependency, a hesitancy to self-disclose, and the tendency to conceal distressing and negative personal information (Komiya, Good, and Sherrod, 2000). Although these behaviors discourage help seeking, they seem to be in line with the military image that is celebrated in the male-dominated military environment. For female soldiers to thrive in this environment, they must adapt their behavior to what is required in a culture that demands rugged individualism coupled with teamwork. Given what we know about the difficulties many female veterans have as they transition back to civilian life (Baechtold and De Sawal, 2009; Holmstedt, 2009), how does their prior military experience affect their ability to seek help? Have they become more like one of the guys in their help-seeking and coping behavior? Do we need to reeducate these women in the importance of and the ways to seek help? These behaviors that limit help seeking confront female and male student veterans, whether they are reentering or entering college for the first time. The nature of the college environment requires a high degree of self-advocacy to successfully deal with a number of new demands, and the ability to use help seeking as a coping strategy is a critical component for success in this academic and social integration process.

Marching Together: Summary

Although a host of challenges face both female and male student veterans as they transition into the college environment, the coping strategies and connectedness that many women establish academically and socially contribute to their success. We know from the data currently available that the rates of MST and PTSD are higher for women and that this discrepancy results in a differential effect for the number of women in the emotional challenges they may face. Seeking help and finding support networks are of particular importance for women who have experienced trauma. For this group of women using help seeking as a coping strategy can be highly effective because of the congruence between care for others as a moral choice and care for self.

The perceptions of mattering and validation are essential to success in the arena of academic challenge for all student veterans and especially for women in a college classroom. Sax, Bryant, and Harper's study (2005) of student-faculty interaction and learning outcomes found differential effects based on gender, with validation, mattering, and connectedness important for women's cognitive and personal development. As female student veterans struggle with developing their sense of identity as learners, the need to form connections with mentors who can assist them in this journey is of primary importance.

Josselson's work (1987) on identity development in women provides helpful insight into understanding this population. In applying her theory to female veterans, it appears that many of these women fall under the identity group that Josselson labels Identity Achievers (Baechtold and De Sawal, 2009; Josselson, 1987). They have grappled with who they are and are paving the way for whom they want to become. They are able to tolerate guilt and disequilibrium, rely on and value their own competence, and display a balance between self and self as related to others. Women in this group demonstrate autonomy and relatedness; it is through the interplay of both that they establish a newly constructed working identity.

Higher education can support female student veterans in a number of ways by capitalizing on the strengths that these women bring to the college environment: developing intentional programming efforts such as mentoring opportunities; establishing learning communities for student veterans; providing a female student veteran group as a subset of the student veterans organization on campus; establishing a link with the counseling center, particularly those that offer family therapy; working with faculty and campus support services by connecting women with programs such as organized study groups, supplemental instruction, and group tutoring; and designing professional development opportunities for faculty to assist them in the classroom so that all women, especially veterans, experience validation as learners and realize that they do matter.

Commentary from Margaret Baechtold
Women Veterans

Margaret Baechtold is a retired lieutenant colonel with twenty years of experience in the U.S. Air Force, where she served as a navigator, executive officer, diplomat, and AFROTC detachment commander. In addition, she has worked for four and one-half years as an academic advisor at Indiana University and since January 2007 as IU's director of veterans support services. Baechtold coauthored a book chapter,

(Continued)

Women Veterans (Continued)

"Meeting the Needs of Women Veterans," in a 2009 edition of New Directions for Student Services. She studied political science and German at the University of Innsbruck, Austria, as an Olmsted Scholar and is a graduate of the Air Command and Staff College and the Armed Forces Staff College.

One of my favorite expressions is that a person is no less a soldier because she is female, and no less a woman because she is a soldier. Women returning to campus from military service are trying to find balance between multiple environments and roles: military/civilian; soldier/student; independent/family member; male-dominated culture/diverse campus culture. Each one will have found a way to personally adapt to military culture, and they will individually react to their unique transition to our civilian campus culture.

One of the most important things for women veterans and service members is to be valued and recognized as individuals—not just as women, not just as veterans, but as themselves and not valued or measured against any stereotypes of either soldiers or females. Some women identify strongly as veterans, and others desire to be seen no differently from civilian women on campus. We try to make campus and our support services and office welcoming to all.

Make no different assumptions about female veterans than you make about male veterans. They may have been exposed to the same combat environment as many men; there is no longer a clear boundary between combat and noncombat assignments. Listen to their individual needs. Some will want to continue their military/veteran role and contacts; others will want to transition to a different student experience. Each is different. But value their service the same. If you plan events or contact individuals, make the same assumptions about service for both men and women. Nothing alienates a female veteran more than seeing staff automatically ask about or recognize military service of men but assume that because they are women, they are not veterans.

Ideas for a Self-Authorship Curriculum for Students with Military Experience

IN FALL 2010, A STUDENT VETERAN attending a community college in Maryland produced a provocative and, from the perspective of school officials, distressing piece of writing for his English class assignment. The student's essay began with the statement that "War is a drug." He continued by describing killing as an addiction and shared some of his darkest feelings about the taking of a human life. At the behest of his English instructor, he submitted the composition to the campus newspaper, where it was subsequently published. Of course, the published essay caused quite an uproar on campus. Two weeks later, the student was barred from campus with the stipulation that he could return after a psychological evaluation was performed and satisfactorily documented. A spokesperson for the college administration said, "He didn't make any direct threats, but we still found some of the content disturbing" and "We have to really be cautious in this post–Virginia Tech world" (Walker, 2010, p. 1). Although public reaction, including from students, was mixed, the reaction by school officials appeared to be reasonable under the circumstances. It is difficult to surmise whether the student veteran's treatise was a therapeutic piece of reflective writing or a desperate cry for help. Not surprisingly, he had been diagnosed with depression, sleep problems, and PTSD. Ultimately, the student chose not to return to the school in question, was making plans to attend elsewhere, and may pursue civil litigation against the community college (Walker, 2010).

The purpose of this chapter is neither to consider the legal ramifications of the Maryland case nor to evaluate the actions of the administrators, faculty, and students. The intention here is to introduce the reader to the notion of creating a place in the college curriculum for students who have served in the conflicts in Iraq and Afghanistan to write frankly about their war service in a safe and confidential environment, thus affording them the opportunity to make meaning of their experiences. The student in the Maryland case stated, "What I'm writing about has nothing to do with the school. Really, it's through writing that I've been able to deal with things" (Walker, 2010, p. 1). (Appendix A includes the full essay.) Having a student "deal with things" through his or her writing is not a novel idea in contemporary higher education. Pennebaker (2004) found that students who invested time writing seriously about the most traumatic events in their lives showed increases in their psychological well-being and demonstrated marked physiological improvements in their immune systems. DeSalvo (1999), in *Writing as a Way of Healing*, described the therapeutic value of writing: "I'd examined my feelings, linked them to something that had happened, and to my past. My feelings of loss . . . no longer overwhelmed me. Now, I felt connected to my feelings and to my life story. . . . I realized, too, that I am committed to writing and the nourishment it provides me" (p. 8). Beyond the healing value of students' writing about their war service, however, is the idea of each individual's drawing meaning from those experiences and using that information to develop his or her sense of values. This notion is particularly interesting when considering the cognitive and affective development of student veterans in college. They come to their college studies with a level of maturity and worldliness that, when compared with traditional-age students, could indicate that little additional cognitive growth and psychosocial development is necessary. This assumption, that a veteran of war is well on his or her way to being a self-actualized adult, is promulgated by the students themselves. Indeed, among the participants in a study by Rumann and Hamrick (2010), one student compared himself with similarly aged students, saying that they "were just a couple of college kids and I'm an experienced combat veteran at this point. . . . I still feel justified in saying that I've got a head start on them emotionally, maturity-wise, life experience-wise" (p. 445). Does this presumed higher level of maturity mean that student veterans should bypass traditional passages of student development such as moving from a dualistic view of the world to one that is increasingly relativistic? Military culture is necessarily dualistic, grounded in external authority, and "by definition must differ significantly from civil culture in a democratic society" (Ulmer and others, 2000, p. 7). The difference is noted in this comment by a twenty-nine-year-old criminal justice major: "I spent eight years in the military, with our own language, our own culture . . . [our] own way of thinking. In the military, they kind of take care of you" (Lawson, 2010, p. 1). Therefore, consider the following scenarios, which were adapted for use with student veterans and developed based on the works of Baxter Magolda (1999, 2007), Baxter Magolda and King (2004), Kegan (1994), Perry (1999), and Pizzalato (2003):

Scenario One: A student veteran reacts to a challenging situation using externally derived absolutes that have been taken from his military experience, where the construction of knowledge is typically not contextual. He does not balance the "military way" of reacting with an internally derived sense of self and personal internal goals because not much exploration of "ways of knowing" or "self-authorship" has occurred.

Scenario Two: A student veteran reacts to the same challenging situation using reasoning skills developed in college, which are based on an understanding that knowledge is contextual in nature and incorporates his important experiences from military service. He balances this cognitive technique for knowing, which has been learned in college, with the development of his own internally defined goals and a sense of self, some of which have been garnered from military experience. This student has some of the cognitive basics down and is now moving toward "self-authorship."

If you were a prospective employer, which of the students would you be more likely to hire based on the scenarios? Maturity and military service do not preclude one from some of the important life lessons learned in college, particularly in the areas of student development and cognitive growth. Whether a traditional-age student or a young adult now home from war service, entering college students' epistemologies are typically dualistic and absolute, because they have been adapted from external sources of authority (parents or the military culture). Under the pretext of higher levels of maturity and the ability to focus, one student noted "that service men and women tend to see school as they see any assignment. . . . The mission comes first. . . . In the military you are taught to keep that in mind above anything else" (Llanos, 2010, p. 1). Another student remarked, "School is a mission to accomplish—my job" (Ely, 2008, p. 1).

Classes for Veterans

Colleges and universities, including the University of Arizona, West Virginia University, and the University of California, Berkeley, are beginning to offer for-credit classes for students with military experience. These types of classes offer students a bit more than the traditional orientation curriculum, which typically familiarizes students with purposes of higher education; identifies essential campus services, resources, and organizations; and presents additional key information for achieving success. Admittedly, some orientation courses address the difficulties in transitioning from military to civilian and college, but the courses at the three schools identified above endeavor to go further, including opportunities for student veterans to write about their wartime experiences and struggles with transition.

The University of Arizona offers four credit-bearing classes that are tailored for cohorts of veterans and provided by the institution's agricultural education department and the Veterans Education and Transfer Services office. For example, AED 210, Resiliency and Human Potential, uses a required curriculum-specific text, *Scholars in Camo*, and "provides a background in resiliency research to foster the knowledge and strategies that enhance resilience" (University of Arizona, 2010, p. 1). The course also uses Frankl's *Man's Search for Meaning* (2006), which is a moving tribute to struggle and perseverance. Journaling and personal reflection are a part of UA's curriculum for student veterans. (Appendix B is a sample of the syllabus used in this course.)

West Virginia University uses a different strategy by tailoring existing courses through sections that are smaller than the traditional enrollment and are specifically for cohorts of veterans. These veteran-only sections are offered in public speaking, English, and history. Interestingly, changes to West Virginia state law in 2010 encouraged these types of classes for veterans. A student affairs official from WVU noted that because "combat makes veterans hypersensitive to their surroundings they need smaller classes with people who've shared the same experiences" (Associated Press, 2010, p. 1). Because writing in the military is often done using fragmented sentence structure with bulleted short briefings, student veterans may seek assistance from WVU's writing center. A graduate student who served in the Army National Guard notes that his first semester in graduate school was much easier because he received assistance to improve his writing, including strategies for combining and expanding ideas (Inks, 2009).

The Student Learning Center at the University of California, Berkeley, offers a one-unit course, Education 198, Veterans in Higher Education. Although the curriculum is similar to traditional orientation classes offered to veterans at schools across the nation, this class is taught by the program director of Reentry Student and Veterans Programs and Services. "When a nontraditional student such as a veteran comes to UC Berkeley, it's not just the individual who benefits, but also his or her family and community, who then see education as an opportunity to advance and impact the world around them" (Anwar, 2008). The presence of this course at UC Berkeley is noteworthy and not without a bit of irony, considering that the campus has been in the national spotlight at various times during the past for antiwar protests, including demonstrations against the Vietnam War and the current conflicts in Iraq and Afghanistan. As part of a statewide "Troops to College" initiative endorsed by the University of California, California State University, and California Community Colleges systems, however, the higher education community in California has pledged to provide support for student veterans (Regus, 2008).

Each of the courses detailed here is in response to the needs of a growing population of student veterans, and the collaborative efforts of administrators, staff, and faculty to create and deliver this sorely needed curriculum are laudable. In the case of the UC Berkeley course, it is notable that the collaboration occurs with both academic affairs and student affairs, between the learning center and veterans services units. None of the courses, however. claim specific learning outcomes related to students' writing about their military experiences, using reflection to make meaning of those experiences, or beginning the process of moving from a military mind-set of external authority and absolutes to one of contextual knowing and self-authorship,

Meaning Making and Self-Authorship

Today's veteran who comes to college after serving in the military during the conflicts in Iraq and Afghanistan brings his or her own suppositions about the nature of knowledge and processes for meaning making. A director at a campus veterans center commented that "a huge [challenging issue] is a lot of these people are coming out of a combat environment without the ability to retune their expectations. [The military trains] them to go to combat, to be aggressive, to respond to violence violently. To retune is sometimes very difficult" (Lawson, 2010, p. 1).

Research about military culture confirms that the ways of knowing for many service personnel while in the service are received from an external authority (Hall, 2008) and dualistic (Amy, 2010; Ulmer and others, 2000). These students may bring to college the belief that there is a single correct answer, a right versus wrong or good versus bad epistemology, in answer to life's complex questions and that answers are usually given by referring to external authority. Ideally, unless significant self-segregation with other veterans occurs throughout their time in college, student veterans move through their collegiate journey becoming increasingly more contextual in their thinking (Baxter Magolda, 1999; Pizzalato, 2003), relativistic in making meaning (Kegan, 1994; Perry, 1999), and see knowledge as constructed (Belenky, Clinchy, Goldberger, and Tarule, 1997; Piaget, 1950). Can the journey toward self-authorship be more intentional for students transitioning from military service to college? One idea for supporting veterans' transition is to create a course that explores these issues through reflection, writing, and discourse.

Concept Mapping for Curriculum Planning

The use of concept mapping to plan a curriculum is both helpful and practical (Lattuca and Stark, 2009). Figure 10 depicts an example concept map for planning the curriculum for a course for students with military experience. This example course is based in a developmental pedagogy and is grounded in the notion that student and instructor will construct and generate knowledge and meaning from their experiences (Kukla, 2000; Piaget, 1950; Vygotsky, 1978). The curriculum

FIGURE 10
Curriculum Concept Map for Creating a College Course for Students with Military Experience

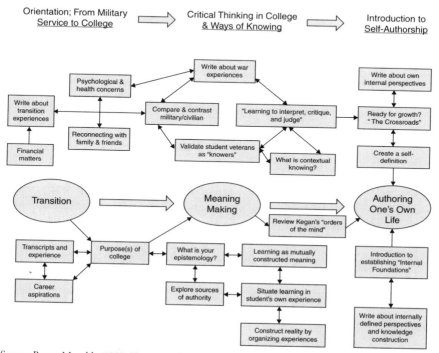

Sources: Baxter Magolda, 1999; Kegan, 1994; Piaget, 1950; Pizzalato, 2003.

is divided into three roughly equal sections: orientation, critical thinking in college and ways of knowing, and introduction to self-authorship. The example depicted in Figure 10 contains enough course content and learning objectives to easily fill a traditional semester-long, three-credit-hour class.

The orientation portion of the course is quite straightforward and covers the material that a traditional class for veterans in transition would receive in a typical one-credit-hour college experience class. The three schools cited earlier are exemplars of the orientation portion by covering issues that students face such as financial matters, psychological and health concerns, personal relationships with friends and family, and the purposes of a college education. From the beginning of the semester students are introduced to the action of writing about their transition experiences. The instructor of a veteran's course offered at Ohio State University says they look for "an environment where active duty students and veterans could engage with material on war without having to deal with any possible stigmas about having students in the class who weren't veterans. . . . We want them to build on their experience and the coursework for the rest of their time at the university. For students who have been through an experience that nobody should have to go through, this should be a good transition into academic work . . . a way for them to take the things they've learned on the ground and apply those resources to their academic experiences" (Epstein, 2009, p. 1).

The second phase of the course is where much of the serious reflective writing occurs. Assignments begin with students' evaluating self in connection with others. At this juncture in the semester, students are asked to write about personal military experiences and analyze what these experiences bring to the challenges and successes they are encountering in their transition to higher education. An assignment might be for students to read a historical novel or a narrative about previous wartime situations and to relate their experiences in combat to what happened in the past. For some veterans, the difficulty will be to feel comfortable enough to integrate personal knowledge, which may be a different way of knowing and thinking about themselves, in relationship to others. It is critical that the instructor establish and honor a safe environment for students to share their thoughts and emotions openly. This approach is in sharp contrast to the scenario described in the introduction to this chapter, where a student's writing was published in the campus newspaper. In class, student veterans are asked to consider complex situations, perhaps in the form of a case study, in which interpretation, critique, and judgment are required (Baxter Magolda, 1999; Baxter Magolda and King, 2004; Sternberg and Grigorenko, 2008). One of the goals here is to introduce students to different sources of authority, constructed knowledge, and contextual decision making (Piaget, 1950). Therefore, the instructor must emphasize that students are "knowers" and that their experiences are valued (Baxter Magolda, 1999).

In the third phase, introduction to self-authorship, students explore various theories and themes in student development such as Chickering and Reisser

(1993), Perry (1999), Josselson (1996), and Baxter Magolda (1999) as well as other applicable resources from the literature on college and transition, including Chickering and Schlossberg (2001) and Schlossberg (2007). A written assignment in this phase might include the selection of one or more theories that seem particularly relevant to the student's development. The writing incorporates an analysis and application of how and why the theory fits and how the knowledge of the theory can help organize experiences they have had.

Another assignment may explore the literature on moral development theory. Moral decisions on a battlefield are of necessity made in a high-intensity, real-life situation, and grappling with them from a civilian mind-set for student veterans most likely presents an enormous struggle. The ability to understand the process and embrace internal perspectives in context is one hallmark of working toward self-authorship. Using Rest's Defining Issues Test (Rest, Narvaez, Bebeau, and Thoma, 1999) and reading and discussing the moral dilemmas of Gilligan (1981) and Kohlberg (1969, 1984) enable students to situate themselves in their own experience and create a definition of who they are and whom they want to become. At this point, students will be ready to work as a team and create their own case studies, based on the literature and their prior knowledge, which allows them to share and engage the class. At this point, the students become the teachers of the course and begin to self-author the curriculum.

The final project in the class incorporates the learning outcomes in Exhibit 1 and provides students the opportunity to participate in mutual critiques. In the large group, class members identify specific problems they feel might be issues on a college campus; for example, the lack of a central location for veterans to go to get answers to questions that are particularly relevant to this population. In a small group, students who elect to work on this project will create a problem statement, research the literature or collect data to support the existence of the problem, determine multiple solutions, and anticipate unintended outcomes to the proposed solutions. The oral part of the project will be presented to the class, with others from the campus or outside community invited if the problem is community focused. The group will prepare an extensive written report based on its findings.

EXHIBIT 1
Example Learning and Development Outcomes for a Self-Authorship Course for Students Transitioning from Military Service to College

Demonstrate through a variety of speaking and writing assignments an increasing self-awareness in the community of the classroom.

Demonstrate the development of independent knowing skills through reflective writing.

Evaluate a coherent sense of self through participation in a classroom team.

Apply multiple strategies to the challenges of transition and higher education.

Explore meaningful interpersonal relationships.

Maintain health and wellness.

Understand and appreciate the concepts of diverse perspectives.

Develop and demonstrate a sense of community responsibility.

Comprehend the depth of knowledge required for a degree.

Conclusion

Faculty members, deans, and other academic affairs administrators are in a unique position to offer a classroom-based developmental approach to dealing with veterans' transition issues that is both educational and scholarly. Courses using the ideas contained in this chapter are often reserved for students attending honors colleges or participating in learning communities. But why not offer this type of developmental coursework to veteran students who bring valuable life experiences to the college classroom? An initiative of this sort should, of course, be led by a well-qualified and skilled faculty member, perhaps someone with a counseling background and military experience.

Traditional orientation curricula that have been adapted to meet the needs of student veterans are an important first step in easing the transition from military service to college attendance. More can be done to assist this emerging student population, however. Classes tailored to help students write about their wartime service, to make meaning of those experiences, and to continue their journey toward developing as an actualized adult and lifelong learner can be a catalyst for a fulfilling and successful transition to civilian life. The pedagogical approach presented in this chapter uses the pathway to self-authorship as a framework for a transition course for student veterans. Other approaches for augmenting and enhancing a college orientation schema for veterans, however, will undoubtedly emerge—an important area for further research. Ultimately, transition courses that can be empirically shown to enhance students' success, both academically and socially, will become the exemplary models for those who endeavor to assist students with military experience.

Commentary from Marcia B. Baxter Magolda
Student Veterans in College

Marcia B. Baxter Magolda is distinguished professor of educational leadership at the Miami University of Ohio and a nationally recognized author and speaker on student development and learning. In 2007 she received the Association for the Study of Higher Education's Research Achievement Award for her outstanding contribution to advancing student learning. Her scholarship addresses the evolution of learning and development in college and subsequent adult life and educational practice to promote self-authorship. Her seventh and eighth books, respectively, are Authoring Your Life and Development and Assessment of Self-Authorship.

1. Dr. Baxter Magolda, what are your general thoughts about student veterans who are attending college after returning from military service?

Before commenting here, I want to emphasize that I have not had the opportunity to work with student veterans. Thus, my comments are in response to the research presented in this chapter and other student development research that suggests that diverse personal characteristics and contextual factors influence young adults' development. It is certainly possible, based on research you summarize here, that some student veterans return having learned to follow external formulas through their military experience. However, dissonance, or experience that calls our ways of making meaning into question, is a key factor in promoting complex meaning making. Some veterans may have experienced this dissonance in their lives prior to military service, and it is reasonable to expect that they experienced pervasive dissonance during their service. Thus, it is possible that their formula following was a strategy for success in the military context. This possibility does not mean that returning is easy, but some may have greater developmental capacity than others to bring to the task. Recognizing a

(Continued)

range of development among veterans will help educators partner with them more effectively to make sense of their experience.

2. How do you see your work in self-authorship as applied to college students with military experience?

Self-authorship, or the capacity to coordinate external influence to internally define one's beliefs, identity, and social relations, enables us to navigate life's challenges more effectively. In times of uncertainty and transition, the internal voice reflected in self-authorship serves as a compass for making sense of experience, crafting who we want to be and how we want to relate to others. As I've described in *Authoring Your Life*, an internal voice helps navigate competing demands in learning, work, and personal life. It also enables people to engage in mutual relationships in which partners authentically negotiate to respect both partners' interests. We know from research that self-authorship helps college students make informed choices about their beliefs, succeed in learning and work, reject negative stereotypes, and enjoy healthy relationships. For student veterans who have the additional challenge of reconstructing their identities and belief systems after their military experience, support in the journey toward self-authorship would help them realize these same benefits.

3. Do you have any recommendations for practitioners who will be working with this emerging population of students?

I have advocated using learning partnerships with all college students; they may be particularly important for student veterans given the challenges they face and the diversity in meaning making that I expect exists among this population. In learning partnerships, educators support students in developing toward self-authorship by respecting their thoughts and feelings so that their voices are valued, helping students use their own experiences as opportunities for growth, and collaborating with learners to solve their own problems. At the same time, educators challenge students by discouraging simple solutions, encouraging learners' personal authority, and working interdependently with learners to solve problems. Student veterans most likely have already come face to face with the complexities of life in ways their peers may never encounter. Helping them process these complexities (rather than avoid them) and bring forward their personal authority, which was likely in the background in military service, are necessary to aid their transition to college and civilian life. The curricular efforts you describe in this chapter reflect characteristics of learning partnerships. Perhaps the greatest strengths of learning partnerships are their connection to learners' individual experience and meaning making as a foundation for the partnership. This would help practitioners working with student veterans to take their cues from the students to determine how to shape the relationship. I have used the metaphor of a tandem bike to explain learning partnerships, suggesting that educators should take the back seat and learners should take the front captain's seat to direct their own journeys. This enables practitioners to affirm and support students' personal authority for their learning and lives.

Institutional Response to an Emerging Population of Veterans

WHAT SORTS OF PROGRAMS, types of services, and forms of support are being offered by colleges and universities in response to the needs of students with military experience? Is empirical evidence available to better inform campus administrators and policymakers who prefer to make data-driven decisions about the programs and services to offer students? The answer is "yes," and using inferential statistics to identify areas of concern is the focus of this chapter.

From Soldier to Student: Easing the Transition of Service Members on Campus (Cook and Kim, 2009), published by the American Council on Education (ACE) and funded by the Lumina Foundation for Education, is the definitive institutional research report on this topic to date. Since 1918, the ACE has provided leadership and a unified voice on key higher education issues. Through advocacy, research, and innovative programs, the ACE represents the interests of more than sixteen hundred campus executives as well as the leaders of higher education associations and organizations. The ACE speaks as higher education's voice in matters of public policy in Washington, D.C., and throughout the nation and provides vital programs, information, and a forum for dialogue on key issues (American Council on Education, 2011a). (The authors wish to thank the ACE for supplying data from *From Student to Soldier* for a secondary analysis, which is used here to provide empirical evidence for policy and planning.)

From Soldier to Student (Cook and Kim, 2009) presents extensive data that examine programs and services that public and private colleges and universities offer to assist students who have military experience in their pursuit of postsecondary education. Findings from the original report are based on information from 723 institutions of higher learning as well as focus group meetings with student veterans. For example, a descriptive finding from the report includes the statistic that only 22 percent of schools serving student veterans provide transition assistance.

To begin the secondary data analysis, including an inferential investigation, an exploratory factor analysis (EFA) using varimax rotation was used (Thompson, 2004). EFA is a useful statistical technique for a secondary analysis of the data from *From Soldier to Student,* because it provides clues for policy consideration such as planning for services, programs, and other institutional supports to assist veterans attending college. This approach is possible because the quantitative results from the EFA show how survey items group or cluster together. For example, institutions that reported providing one program or service for a particular question in the survey also tended to provide others, and those relationships are indicated by the EFA factor groupings. This technique, often implemented in Q-methodology policy research, is applicable here because the factor analysis "clusters can be interpreted as policy narratives. The elegance of this method is that it is not sensitive to the narratives that the analyst *a priori* expects to be there" (Fischer and Miller, 2007, p. 258). For purposes of analysis, a binary scoring scheme is used whereby, for each institutional participant's response to a nondemographic question, either a value of one was assigned (if answered in the affirmative) or a zero was assigned. Using ones and zeros as binary values in variable columns is ideal for the varimax rotation approach, because the output tends to produce high factor loadings closer to plus or minus one (Martinez and Martinez, 2005).

Findings from the secondary analysis of the *From Soldier to Student* data yielded five factors, which can be thought of as areas of focus for use by institutional decision makers for policy consideration. Note that nearly two-thirds (65.6 percent) of the variance in the entire study can be explained by the five factors, which have been named and labeled by the authors as Financial Matters, Administrative and Strategic Planning, Advising and Career Services, Psychological Counseling Services, and Veterans Office on Campus. Kachigan (1991) suggests that the interpretation and labeling of factor loadings should be based on the subject-matter knowledge of the researcher and combined with what is already known about the topic, thus increasing reliability and comprehensibility. The results of the EFA showing the factor loadings for each question are provided in Exibit 1.

Before moving forward with a closer inspection of the five factors, it is important to establish the statistical impact that the percentage of total student body enrollment of military veterans has on the *From Soldier to Student* survey responses. After all, why would a school with very low, or perhaps no, enrollment of students with military experience endeavor to offer programs and services? And, indeed, this is the case. Figure 11 shows the positive correlation between percentage of enrollment of veterans and military students and number of affirmative answers about programs and services on the ACE survey. The relationship is positive and statistically significant ($r_{(668)}$ = 0.202, $p < 0.001$).

To get a better visual inspection of the data for those schools with low enrollment, Figure 12 was created. Notice in the figure that in the area marked by the oval shape, many of the institutions that reported low percentages of enrollment of veterans and military personnel also reported very low or no affirmative answers—five or fewer and often zero—to the questions about providing programs and services in the survey. If this is the case, should those schools be included in further analysis as they are not yet "in the game" with respect to providing support for students with military experience because of low enrollment?

For the analysis provided in this chapter, we established a cutoff of one-half of one percent enrollment (<0.5 percent). Therefore, only colleges and universities with percentage enrollments of veterans of one-half percent or greater were included in subsequent analysis. Doing so lowered the total sample size to $N = 576$ and in a sense excluded "outliers" from the data set but left a sufficient number of institutions for a robust analysis. Moreover, the research method employed included the use of two grouping variables from the survey, educational sector and percentage enrollment of veterans and military students. The educational sector was coded to delineate three groups: public four-year colleges and universities (n = 211), private four-year colleges and universities (n = 167), and public two-year colleges (n = 198). The other grouping variable, percentage of enrollment, was also coded for three groups: 0.5 percent to less than 1 percent (0.5 to <1 percent, n = 106), 1 percent to

EXHIBIT 1

Exploratory Factor Analysis Results from Secondary Data Analysis of the *From Soldier to Student* Survey

Survey Question	Financial Matters	Admin Planning	Advising/ Career	Counseling	Veterans Office
Q11 h. VA education benefits counseling	**0.607**	0.277	0.325	0.266	0.202
Q13b. Credits for military training according to ACE	**0.730**	0.291	0.323	0.069	0.121
Q13c. Credits for military occupation according to ACE	**0.680**	0.269	0.301	−0.092	0.121
Q24. Established policy for tuition reimbursement	**0.687**	0.261	0.259	0.193	0.142
Q26d. In-state tuition for veterans (maintain home)	**0.764**	0.140	0.040	0.249	0.120
Q26e. In-state tuition for veterans (assigned to state)	**0.797**	0.092	0.051	0.297	0.203
Q26f. In-state tuition for dependents (assigned to state)	**0.786**	0.086	0.013	0.251	0.205
Q4. Are programs part of long-term planning?	0.317	**0.555**	0.268	0.046	0.009
Q5c. Increased budget for veterans services	0.054	**0.783**	0.395	0.120	0.013
Q5d. Increased number of veterans programs	0.147	**0.785**	0.061	0.144	0.011
Q5e. Increased staff for services and programs	0.099	**0.716**	0.055	0.194	0.115
Q5h. Professional development for faculty/staff	0.145	**0.562**	0.073	0.166	0.079
Q10b. Increased emphasis on new programs/services	0.221	**0.511**	0.142	0.232	0.293
Q10c. Increased emphasis on marketing/communications	0.235	**0.570**	0.232	−0.009	0.236

Q11a. Academic advising available for veterans	0.222	0.151	**0.827**	0.085	0.154
Q11b. Academic support available for veterans	0.133	0.123	**0.866**	0.102	0.027
Q11d. Career planning/services for veterans	0.080	0.112	**0.837**	0.162	0.074
Q11e. Employment assistance for veterans	0.303	0.139	**0.583**	0.309	0.270
Q16b. Staff specifically for veterans with disabilities	0.088	0.220	0.168	**0.721**	0.178
Q16g. Staff trained to assist students with brain injuries	0.142	0.131	0.120	**0.711**	0.045
Q17e. Provide assistance for social adjustment, more	0.379	0.189	0.116	**0.670**	−0.003
Q18c. Coordinate with US Dept. Veterans Affairs	0.394	0.253	0.140	**0.570**	0.174
Q19. Veterans office specifically for this population	0.353	0.187	0.216	0.165	**0.813**
Q20. Veterans office provides services for family	0.283	0.162	0.136	0.129	**0.860**
Variance explained by the factors:	19.3%	14.9%	13.1%	10.3%	8.0%
Total variance explained	**65.6%**				

Note: Shaded scores show question's factor grouping.

FIGURE 11
**Scatter Plot of the Correlation Between Percentage Enrollment
of Student Veterans and Number of Affirmative Answers to the
From Soldier to Student Survey**

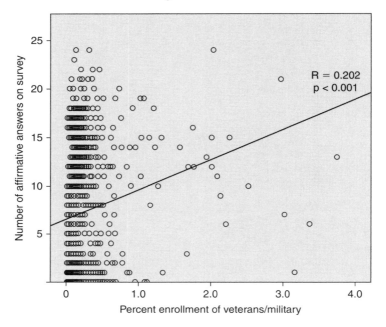

less than 3 percent (1 to <3 percent, n = 286), and 3 percent or greater
(3 percent or >, n = 184).

The chi-square test of Pearson (1932) was chosen as the statistical technique for inferential analysis of the survey items, which were all classified as
nonparametric, categorical data (Greenwood and Nikulin, 1996). Chi-square
analysis using the aforementioned two grouping variables—educational sector and percentage of enrollment—was performed on each of the survey items
that made up the five factors from the EFA (Exhibit 1). Because nearly all the
items analyzed were statistically significant at the $p = 0.05$ level, a level of practical significance was established using a Cramer's V coefficient, a measure of
association that has values between 0, or zero association, and 1, perfect association (Howell, 2002). Only those analyses that equaled or exceed a Cramer's

FIGURE 12

Scatter Plot Showing How Few Affirmative Answers to Survey Items Were Given by Schools with the Lowest Percentages of Enrollment of Veterans and Military Personnel

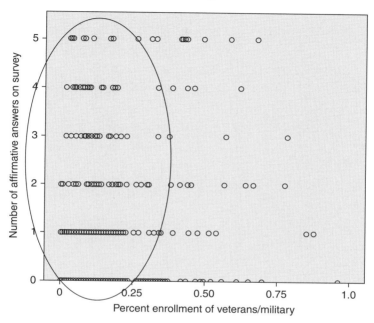

V coefficient of 0.20 were included in the findings. Results for EFA Factor One (Financial Matters) and EFA Factor Two (Administrative and Strategic Planning) are shown in Exhibit 2.

EFA Factor One—Financial Matters

Differences of practical significance in the survey items reported in Exhibit 2 for Factor One were all based on educational sector, none on percentage of enrollment, and two findings in particular are of interest. The first item of significance is the survey question related to accepting certain types of military training, including from military schools, for evaluated college credits. Private four-year colleges and universities were statistically less likely to accept military training for college credits (35 percent) when compared with public

EXHIBIT 2

Differences of Practical Significance in Survey Items for EFA Factors One and Two

Differences of practical significance in survey items from the ACE *From Soldier to Student study* (Cook & Kim, 2009) differentiated by 'educational sector' and by 'percent enrollment of military/veterans' for EFA Factors One and Two.

Factor One – Financial Matters

Item from ACE survey (differentiated by educational sector)	Chi-square, Significance, Cramer's V	Interpretation (magnitude in parentheses)
13.b. School accepts evaluated credit for military training	$\chi^2_{(2, N = 576)} = 23.81, p < 0.001, V = 0.20$	Private 4-year schools were significantly less likely to accept credits (moderate)
24. Policy regarding tuition refunds for deployments or activation	$\chi^2_{(2, N = 576)} = 55.41, p < 0.001, V = 0.31$	Private 4-year schools were significantly less likely to offer tuition refund (strong)
26.d. In-state tuition for those who maintain state as home of record	$\chi^2_{(2, N = 576)} = 96.42, p < 0.001, V = 0.41$	Private 4-year schools were significantly less likely to offer in-state tuition (very strong)
26.e. In-state tuition for those assigned to the state	$\chi^2_{(2, N = 576)} = 104.45, p < 0.001, V = 0.43$	Private 4-year schools were significantly less likely to offer in-state tuition (very strong)
26.f. In-state tuition for dependents of those stationed in the state	$\chi^2_{(2, N = 576)} = 86.35, p < 0.001, V = 0.39$	Private 4-year schools were significantly less likely to offer tuition for dependents (very strong)

Factor Two – Administrative & Strategic Planning

Item from ACE survey	Chi-square, Significance, Cramer's V	Interpretation (magnitude in parentheses)
(differentiated by % enrollment of military/veterans)		
4. Are programs/services part of with long-term strategic plan?	$\chi^2_{(2, N = 576)} = 30.33$, $p < 0.001$, $V = 0.23$	Significantly larger proportion of schools low % enroll did not (moderate)
(differentiated by educational sector)		
4. Are programs/services part of answered long-term strategic plan?	$\chi^2_{(2, N = 576)} = 22.89$, $p < 0.001$, $V = 0.20$	Significant # of private 4-yr schools 'no' or 'don't know' (moderate)
5.d. Next 5 years–increase number yr of veterans services and programs?	$\chi^2_{(2, N = 576)} = 34.07$, $p < 0.001$, $V = 0.24$	Significant # of both public 2-yr & private 4-schools did not check this box (moderate)
5.e. Next 5 years–increase staff for veterans programs and services?	$\chi^2_{(2, N = 576)} = 24.05$, $p < 0.001$, $V = 0.20$	Significant # of private 4-yr schools did not check this box (moderate)

two-year (55 percent) and public four-year (60 percent) institutions. Regardless of sector or type of school a veteran chooses to attend, the issue of a fair evaluation of military training to award college credits is important to students with military experience but can also be confusing for an untrained college advisor. One of several college administrators interviewed by Persky (2010) characterized the transcript process this way: The student veteran "shows up with 10 transcripts of all these schools they've gone to in the last 10 years and what is supposed to happen is the advisor who understands this system and who one would hope is committed to helping veterans, sits down with them, does an interview, and then spends some time alone with these ACE guides doing the evaluation. It's not hard to do, but you have to be trained to do it" (p. 82). Campus personnel need to be aware that training is the key for assisting veterans in transcript evaluation. Information about resources and training for academic advisors is available from both the American Council on Education (2011b) and the Servicemembers Opportunity Colleges (2010).

Another finding of interest from the data analysis regards the tuition refund policy for students who experience military activations and deployments during a semester. Private four-year schools were statistically less likely to have a tuition refund policy (26 percent) when compared with both the public community colleges and public four-year schools, 53 percent and 65 percent, respectively. In fairness to the private institutions, many of them have just in the past year or so experienced growth in their student veteran populations and are likely exploring the options regarding supports and policies such as tuition refunds. One private university that does have policies regarding deployment, the University of Notre Dame, according to a guide published by the Military Family Research Institute (Sternberg, Wadsworth, Vaughan, and Carlson, 2009), demonstrates considerable institutional flexibility to service members by deeming, among various scenarios, that "if deployment occurs earlier in term, full withdrawal with full tuition refund may be best outcome" (p. 120).

The final three items of practical significance shown in Exhibit 2 all deal with question 26 and various scenarios and policies for granting in-state tuition for active-duty service personnel and their dependents. Once again, the private institutions were statistically identified as an anomaly, but this question is probably moot because in-state tuition policies really have no bearing on the tuition structure at these schools. Therefore, campus officials charged with creating policies for the student veteran populations on their campuses should take note of the two main Factor One issues raised in this section: college credits for military training and tuition refund policies.

EFA Factor Two—Administrative and Strategic Planning

Practical differences of significance occurred in both grouping variables, "percent of enrollment of student veterans" and "educational sector," for Factor Two. The survey item indicating whether an institution was engaged in long-term strategic planning to provide services and programs for veterans is of particular interest in this chapter, which is aimed at informing administrators and policymakers. Schools in the sample that had between 0.5 and less than 1 percent of total enrollment were statistically significantly less likely to answer affirmatively (52 percent) regarding long-range planning than institutions with enrollments of 1 percent and higher (74 percent). This situation is worrisome, because the lower-enrollment schools are the colleges and universities that should be engaging in long-term strategic planning, as, depending on the operational requirements of the military, potentially tens of thousands of veterans will be returning home over the next few years and many of them will be enrolling at these very institutions. Will they be ready?

The same survey item about planning showed practical significance when grouped by educational sector. Four-year private schools were statistically less likely to answer affirmatively (49 percent) when compared with public two-year colleges (67 percent) and public four-year institutions (72 percent). When considering this finding along with the previous one, it is reasonable to surmise that four-year private schools are doing less strategic planning in anticipation of providing programs and services for students with military experience. This finding was confirmed using a post hoc chi-square analysis comparing low-enrollment schools across the educational sectors. Four-year private institutions with low enrollment of veterans were significantly less likely to answer affirmatively about long-term strategic planning (33 percent) than the lower-enrollment public two-year and public four-year schools, 56 percent and 67 percent, respectively. The finding exceeded the Cramer's V threshold and thus was practically significant ($\chi^2_{(2, N = 129)} = 11.28$, $p = 0.004$, $V = 0.30$).

Yellow Ribbon is a federal program in which colleges and universities "fund tuition expenses that exceed the highest public in-state undergraduate tuition rate. The institution can contribute up to 50 percent of those expenses and VA will match the same amount as the institution" (U.S. Department of Veterans Affairs, 2009c, p. 1). Ignoring planning for this emerging student population could be troublesome. Private schools that participate in the program can expect an increase in veteran enrollments and should be engaging in long-term strategic planning to consider how best to assist students with military experience to succeed.

Similar to the question about strategic planning (and shown in Exhibit 2), participants were also asked about plans for the next five years. For example, when asked if they were considering increasing the number of veterans service and programs (Question 5.d), only 32 percent of private four-year schools and 40 percent of public two-year colleges answered affirmatively, which was practically significant when compared with four-year public colleges and universities (60 percent). The next item asked about considering increasing staff for veterans program and services in the next five years. For this item, a significantly lower percentage of private four-year schools answered affirmatively (19 percent) when compared with both the public two-year and public four-year institutions, at 28 percent and 42 percent, respectively. Overall, the findings for Factor Two—Administrative and Strategic Planning indicate that colleges and universities, both public and private, should be engaging in planning to meet the needs of an emerging population of students with military experience.

EFA Factor Three—Advising and Career Services

As noted in Exhibit 3, statistical differences of interest occurred in Factor Three by both "educational sector" and "percent of enrollment of student veterans." For example, schools with low veteran enrollment (0.5 to <1 percent total enrollment) were statistically less likely to offer academic advising specifically to meet the needs of students with military experience. Only 10 percent of these institutions reported providing academic advising for veterans versus 33 percent of schools with higher enrollments, which is not surprising because low enrollment has not signaled that any special initiatives be pursued in this area. Schools experiencing rapid enrollment growth of student veterans and the campus administrators tasked with academic affairs responsibilities may want to keep the issue of academic advising in the fore. Ely (2008) surmises that "college advisers working with former service members should draw upon the military member's past experience. Keep the veterans focused on how the skills they acquired in the military are transferable to civilian life" (p. 1).

Another item of interest from the survey was Question 11.e, which asked whether the responding institution offered employment assistance specifically for veterans such as the federally funded VA work study program (U.S. Department of Veterans Affairs, 2009b), traditional student work study, on-campus employment, or job placement for off-campus employment. Private four-year colleges and universities were statistically less likely to offer employment assistance (11 percent) when compared with public two-year (35 percent) and public four-year (43 percent) institutions. Braxton noted in his earlier commentary that on-campus employment would be an excellent way to help student veterans become part of the campus community. At San Diego State University, staff members from the veterans center assist students in finding on-campus jobs (Jacobs, 2009).

EFA Factor Four—Psychological Counseling Services

Differences of practical significance reported in Exhibit 3 for Factor Four were all based on the educational sector. For example, less than 8 percent of the private four-year colleges and universities (thirteen out of 167) reported having someone on staff who is trained in working with veterans with disabilities (Question 16.b), which was significantly lower than for public four-year (28.9 percent) and public two-year (20.7 percent) schools. As more students

EXHIBIT 3

Differences of Practical Significance in Survey Items for EFA Factors Three, Four, and Five

Differences of practical significance in survey items from the ACE *From Soldier to Student* study (Cook & Kim, 2009) differentiated by 'percent enrollment of military/veterans' and by 'educational sector' for EFA Factors Three, Four, and Five.

Factor Three – Advising & Career Services

Item from ACE survey	Chi-square, Significance, Cramer's V	Interpretation (magnitude in parentheses)
(differentiated by % enrollment of military/veterans)		
11.a. Specifically offer academic advising for veterans/military?	$\chi^2_{(2,N=576)} = 25.35, p < 0.001, V = 0.21$	Schools w/low enrollment (0.5 to <1%) less likely to provide advising (moderate)
(differentiated by educational sector)		
11.e. Specifically offer employment assistance for veterans/military?	$\chi^2_{(2,N=576)} = 48.12, p < 0.001, V = 0.29$	Private 4-yr schools were significantly less likely to provide employment assist (mod.–strong)

Factor Four – Psychological Counseling Services

Item from ACE survey	Chi-square, Significance, Cramer's V	Interpretation (magnitude in parentheses)
(differentiated by educational sector)		
16.b. Have staff member specifically trained for veterans w/disabilities?	$\chi^2_{(2,N=576)} = 26.14, p < 0.001, V = 0.21$	Private 4-yr schools were significantly less likely to have disabilities specialist (mod.)

Item	Chi-square, Significance, Cramer's V	Interpretation (magnitude in parentheses)
17.e. Provide counseling for combat veterans?	$\chi^2_{(2, N=576)} = 60.55$, $p < 0.001$, $V = 0.32$	Significant # of both public 2-yr & private 4-yr schools did not provide this type (strong)
18.c. Coordinate w/Veterans Administration?	$\chi^2_{(2, N=576)} = 41.11$, $p < 0.001$, $V = 0.27$	Private 4-yr schools were significantly less likely to coordinate with VA (mod.–strong)

Factor Five – Veterans Office on Campus

Item from ACE survey (differentiated by % enrollment of military/veterans)	Chi-square, Significance, Cramer's V	Interpretation (magnitude in parentheses)
19. Have dedicated veterans office?	$\chi^2_{(2, N=576)} = 21.92$, $p < 0.001$, $V = 0.20$	Low enrollment 0.5 to <1% did not (moderate)
20. Veterans office supports families?	$\chi^2_{(2, N=576)} = 29.94$, $p < 0.001$, $V = 0.22$	Low enrollment 0.5 to <1% did not (moderate)
(differentiated by educational sector)		
19. Have dedicated veterans office?	$\chi^2_{(2, N=576)} = 42.03$, $p < 0.001$, $V = 0.27$	4-yr private schools less likely (mod.-strong)
20. Veterans office supports families?	$\chi^2_{(2, N=576)} = 22.66$, $p < 0.001$, $V = 0.20$	4-yr private schools less likely (moderate)

with military experience enroll in private schools, especially as the result of programs such as Yellow Ribbon, a shortage of specially trained staff to work with students with disabilities could become problematic for all postsecondary educational sectors as the result of an anticipated enrollment of 2 million veterans in higher education (American Council on Education, 2008). According to Grossman (2009, p. 4): "An estimate of 40 percent [veterans with disabilities] is not unreasonable given the reported prevalence in the military and VA medical systems of OEF/OIF veterans identified with post traumatic stress disorder . . . , traumatic brain injury . . . , depression, substance abuse, hearing and vision related injuries, substantial mobility limitations owing to brain and orthopedic injuries, as well as disfiguring burns and debilitating toxic exposure (Church, 2009; National Academy of Sciences, 2008; Rand Corporation, 2008)."

Another item of interest from the ACE survey is Question 17.e regarding the provision of campus-based counseling for combat veterans who suffer from PTSD, depression, and other psychological difficulties. Of public community colleges and four-year private schools, only 26 percent and 19 percent, respectively, reported providing this service when compared with public four-year institutions (54 percent). From an administrative perspective, this situation is understandable because of the lack of resources, particularly for two-year schools. Providing this type of specialized counseling on campus is expensive and may be cost prohibitive for many institutions. What can be done to address this need?

Interestingly, the next survey item shown in Exhibit 3, Question 18.c, "Coordinating with the Veterans Administration," hints at providing a solution to the counseling problem. The U.S. Department of Veterans Affairs plans to expand a pilot program called VetSuccess, which places "counselors and outreach coordinators from VA's Vet Centers . . . to campuses to provide vocational testing, career and academic counseling, and readjustment counseling services" (2010, p. 1). The idea of outsourcing counseling to the VA to provide on-campus services could be a viable solution, particularly for the four-year private and two-year public educational sectors. It is incumbent on campus administrators to reach out to the VA, establish a working relationship, and request direct on-campus support from the agency.

EFA Factor Five—Veterans Office on Campus

Similar to Factor Three and as indicated in Exhibit 3, statistical differences of interest occur in Factor Five by both percentage of enrollment of student veterans and educational sector. For example, schools with low veteran enrollment and private four-year institutions were statistically less likely to provide a dedicated office on campus for serving veterans at 21 percent and 13 percent, respectively. This situation is in contrast to schools with 1 percent or more veteran enrollments (40 percent) and the two-year and four-year public institutions (40 percent). This finding is reasonable when considering that schools with lower veteran enrollments are perhaps beginning to recognize the needs of this emerging student population and would not as of yet created a dedicated office. Interestingly, even state legislatures such as in Minnesota (State of Minnesota, 2010) and Washington (Washington State Legislature, 2011) are getting involved in requiring dedicated veterans offices at state colleges and universities. More than a place for veterans to connect and interact, a single point-of-contact veterans office on campus "serves as a place to start navigating the bureaucracy of higher education" (Klein, 2010, p. 1).

The campus office for student veterans can also serve as a resource for the families of student veterans. Question 20 from the survey asked whether this same office or department provides services for family members of service members and veterans. Overall, 33 percent of the total sample (all educational sectors included) answered in the affirmative regarding assistance for families. Schools with low student veteran enrollment and the four-year private institutions were statistically less likely to offer this service at 15 percent and 11 percent, respectively. At Arkansas State University, staff at the campus center for veterans emphasize family support. According to the center's director, "We have two Thursday night meetings a month to show our support to the students' families. It is a very unique program. We are the only school in Arkansas that has a support system for the veterans and their families. We are trying to encourage other universities to start a support system for the families" (Kaberline, 2010, p. 1). Administrators and others tasked with planning for services on campus can consider the need for a one-stop center for student veterans on their campuses, particularly if this population increases to 1 percent or more of the student enrollment.

Conclusion

From Soldier to Student (Cook and Kim, 2009) provides an invaluable source for investigating issues related to the increased numbers of student veterans on college campuses across the nation and the responses that institutions have made in terms of policies, programs, and services. The goal of this chapter was to provide an empirical resource of information necessary for campus administrators and policymakers to use to make data-driven decisions about this emerging issue in higher education. Several areas were identified as starting points for considering where to dedicate scarce resources to the effort.

Financial matters, including problems with tuition refunds and transcript evaluation, were identified as issues for investigation at each campus, as were tasks associated with strategic planning and administration. Moreover, academic advising and career services were pinpointed as units where increased support for student veterans should be considered. One critical area, psychological and counseling services, should be addressed as soon as possible at each campus, because increasing numbers of students may come to campus with physical or psychological injuries. Finally, a one-stop veterans' support office is recommended for institutions that have the wherewithal to dedicate physical space, focus support, and marshal resources.

Concluding Thoughts

"WAR IS A DRUG" IS THE BOLD QUOTATION that opens *The Hurt Locker*, a film about an Army sergeant and his ordnance disposal team in Iraq. We use this fictional narrative as a qualitative tool in this volume to help the reader better understand the phenomenon of the returning combat veteran. It is noteworthy to mention that this comment was also the opening sentence in the student essay shown in Appendix A. As a generalization describing the psychological effects of combat, this observation about the addictive nature of war as well as other scenes from the movie depicting the struggles some returning veterans face might not be accurate for a majority of men and women who have served, but it does provide an example for college professionals to consider when seeking to assist this student population. In the movie, the drug-like effect of combat helps to explain why the main character, Sergeant James, would desire to return to Iraq after his tour of duty is complete, despite leaving a wife and child behind at home. Ironically, James finds comfort in the war zone, where he has a sense of purpose and meaning in life, in contrast to his perceived anonymity and disappointment in his civilian existence. One element of transition from military service to civilian life for many returning veterans is the quest to find or rediscover purpose and meaning. Interestingly, the pursuit of a college education can become an ideal activity for self-discovery and making meaning. Higher education officials, armed with a fundamental understanding of the issues faced by the student veteran population on their campuses, can provide sorely needed assistance in this transition. That is one of the overarching themes of this monograph.

We wish to thank those who so graciously agreed to provide commentaries about student veterans and college. It is remarkable how accurate these knowledgeable higher education professionals were in raising some of the key issues that students who come to college from military service face, even if they have no direct experience with this student population. We hope the reader is inspired from this wise counsel as much as we are. So where do those of us interested in this topic go from here?

The first "wave" of research on this topic, conducted over the past five years or so since 2007, is coming to a close. Important findings from this past period include evidence that peer connections and support are initially vital for early student success and that institutions should, if enrollment numbers justify it and where practicable, introduce a "one-stop shop" approach to veterans services. And even when resources are not available or large populations of veterans are not present on campus, colleges and universities can at the very least create a virtual version of the one-stop shop by organizing their Web sites to include a user-friendly, dedicated page for students coming to their institutions from military service. A research project investigating the number and value of these sorts of Internet resources for veterans would be helpful.

For example, during the second wave over the next five years from 2012 to 2017, research ideas grounded in existing theory and previously published empirical studies from the general higher education literature, including the examples presented in this volume, are a logical place to begin. Longitudinal studies of persistence and student success are now possible as veterans matriculate year by year on their collegiate journeys. If you are a researcher or administrator who partners with an institutional research office at your institution or elsewhere, make certain that veteran status is collected as a variable at the individual student record level, which will make future studies possible, particularly larger-scale quantitative investigations. As both Astin and Braxton pointed out in their commentaries, it is logical to think that veterans could thrive at commuter institutions versus residential settings, which is something that should be studied further and framed using outcomes such as persistence, elements of the student experience, and degree attainment. Moreover, we anticipate that there will be statistically significant differences between subpopulations of student veterans and other groups, including the general student population. What about delivery of instruction via the Internet and online learning for this special population? Apparently, it is a popular option for these students; more research in this area is needed. Exploring these sorts of issues and providing solid empirical evidence will assist administrators and practitioners with decision making about services, supports, and programs. Additionally, the research focus will shift from access to degree attainment. These are examples of where the next phase of research about veterans in college is heading.

Ideas about providing transition assistance and courses designed to help students with military ties deal with the future (and the past) are intriguing. We know that many of these students are coming to school underprepared and with burdens. As Schlossberg pointed out in her commentary, "For some of these veterans, they can't clear their minds of what they've been through to focus on the textbook they're supposed to be reading or the paper they're supposed to be writing." An orientation curriculum geared toward mitigating these difficulties is something that many colleges and universities could accommodate. Research in this area of transition and adjustment, likely using qualitative methods, is fascinating and will no doubt be part of this next period of research on the student veteran phenomenon.

The latest statistics about how many of our military men and women have physical disabilities, invisible psychological injuries, or both, are alarming. If left unaddressed or untreated, those who suffer from these difficulties will start their college journey at a severe disadvantage, which will greatly affect their chances for academic success. Are campus disability offices and counseling centers prepared for increased numbers of students who will require accommodations and assistance, especially when these services are already stretched thin at some institutions? Obviously, a sense of urgency surrounds this particular issue, an area of investigation that is timely in terms of the need for empirical findings now to inform campus decision makers.

The famous rocket engineer Werner von Braun once remarked that "Research is what I'm doing when I don't know what I'm doing." We hope this volume inspires readers, both practitioners and researchers, to discover constructive ways in which to assist the new generation of veterans who are attending college in greater numbers. These students are the men and women who have served our country during times of conflict, and we in the higher education community can do our part to support their noble desire to pursue a college education.

Appendix A: A Veteran's essay

The following is the essay that Iraq war veteran Charles Whittington wrote for his English class at the Community College of Baltimore County. It was published in the campus newspaper October 26, 2010:

War is a drug. When soldiers enter the military from day one, they begin to train and are brain washed to fight and to handle situations in battle. We train and train for combat, and then when we actually go to war, it is reality and worse than what we have trained for. We suffer through different kinds of situations. The Army never taught how to deal with our stress and addictions. War is a drug because when soldiers are in the Infantry, like me, they get used to everything, and fast. I got used to killing and after a while it became something I really had to do. Killing becomes a drug, and it is really addictive. I had a really hard time with this problem when I returned to the United States, because turning this addiction off was impossible. It is not like I have a switch I can just turn off. To this day, I still feel the addictions running through my blood and throughout my body, but now I know how to keep myself composed and keep order in myself, my mind. War does things to me that are so hard to explain to someone that does not go through everything that I went through. That's part of the reason why I want to go back to war so badly, because of this addiction. Over in Iraq and Afghanistan killing becomes a habit, a way of life, a drug to me and to other soldiers like me who need to feel like we can survive off of it. It is something that I do not just want, but something I really need so I can feel like myself. Killing a man and looking into his eyes, I see his soul draining from his body; I am taking away his life for the harm he has caused me, my family, my country. Killing is a drug to me and has been ever since the first time I have killed someone. At first, it was weird and felt wrong, but by the time of the third and fourth killing it feels so natural. It feels like I could do this for the rest of my life and it makes me happy. There are several addictions in war, but this one is mine. This is what I was trained to do and now I cannot get rid of it; it will be with me for the rest of my life and hurts me that I cannot go back to war and kill again, because I would love to. When I stick my blade through his stomach or his ribs or slice his throat it's a feeling that I cannot explain, but feels so good to me, and I become addicted to seeing and acting out this act of hate, and violence against the rag heads that hurt our country. Terrorists will have nowhere to hide because there are hundreds of thousands of soldiers like me who feel like me and want their revenge as well.

Appendix B: Example Syllabus

University of Arizona
Agricultural Education Department
AED 210: Resiliency and Human Potential

Academic Year: Spring 2010
Instructors: Callahan and Marks

Required Texts: *Scholars in Camo, Peak Performance Through Nutrition and Exercise,* Singh, Bennett, and Deuster (PDF online), *Man's Search for Meaning,* Viktor E. Frankl (PDF online)

Meeting: 300PM–415PM, Mondays and Wednesdays

Description: The course provides a background in resiliency research to foster the knowledge and strategies that enhance resilience. Specific focus is on research-based resiliency methods, assessment, and the physical, psychological, and social systems of resiliency.

Goal: The goal of this course is to understand, assess, plan, and apply resiliency practices that manage stress in a manner that fosters academic, personal, and professional development.

Course Objectives: Detailed, by session, in *Scholars in Camo.*

Expectations: This course is a research-based curriculum requiring a high level of participant commitment. The expectation is that you will maintain a comprehensive journal, provide written commentary, complete activities and participate in discussions on research and readings.

Participation and Evaluation: Every course objective has an associated activity requiring your attention. Writing is coupled with every session. You are expected to maintain a journal. The journal contents are closely integrated with your readings and group discussions requiring that you respond to the journal's subject material in a timely manner.

Although the journal is your personal work, it will be spot-checked in class to assure it is up to date. Additional written components, beyond the journal, will typically involve 200- to 500-word commentary. And, you will be expected to write commentary reflective of your previous written commentary so as to provide comparative measures of change in your learning.

Specific major activities of note include development of a resilience plan, development of a nutrition plan, development of an exercise plan, reflective essay from a book reading, and obtaining and maintaining baseline and ongoing evaluative measures.

Course Activities

Journal: (80%) Maintain your journal in a timely manner consistent with the syllabus. Complete activities, provide 200- to 500-word commentaries and participate in related group discussions.

Reflective Writing: (10%) You will be expected to compose a reflective essay from a book reading.

Mid-term and Final Evaluations: (10%) There will be a mid-term and final evaluations that will require you to evaluate and reflect on your course learning.

References

Abes, E. S., Jones, S. R., and McEwen, M. K. (2007). Reconceptualizing the model of multiple dimensions of identity: The role of meaning-making capacity in the construction of multiple identities. *Journal of College Student Development, 48,* 1–22.

Ackerman, R., DiRamio, D., and Garza Mitchell, R. L. (2009). Transitions: Combat veterans as college students. *New Directions for Student Services, 126,* 5–14.

Allen, D., and Haynie, J. (2008). Beyond yellow ribbons: Higher education comes to the aid of veterans. *Student Affairs Leader, 36*(23), 1–5.

Alvarez, L. (2008, November 2). Combat to college. *The New York Times—Education Life* (online). Retrieved September 24, 2010, from www.nytimes.com/2008/11/02/education/edlife/vets.html.

Ambrose, S. E. (1992). *Band of brothers: E Company, 506th Regiment, 101st Airborne. From Normandy to Hitler's Eagle's Nest.* New York: Simon & Schuster.

American Council on Education. (2008). Serving those who serve: Higher education and America's veterans. *ACE* (online). Retrieved February 3, 2011, from http://www.acenet.edu/Content/NavigationMenu/ProgramsServices/MilitaryPrograms/serving/Veterans_Issue_Brief_1108.pdf.

American Council on Education. (2011a). About ACE. *ACE* (online). Retrieved February 12, 2011, from www.acenet.edu/AM/Template.cfm?Section=About_ACE.

American Council on Education. (2011b). ACE Military Programs. *ACE* (online). Retrieved February 9, 2011, from www.acenet.edu/AM/Template.cfm?Section=Military_Programs.

Amy, L. E. (2010). *The wars we inherit: Military life, gender violence, and memory.* Philadelphia: Temple University Press.

Antonio, A. L. (2004). The influence of friendship groups on intellectual self-confidence and educational aspirations in college. *Journal of Higher Education, 75*(4), 446–471.

Anwar, Y. (2008, June 23). Campus rolls out red carpet for veterans. *UC Berkeley News* (online). Retrieved February 2, 2011, from berkeley.edu/news/media/releases/2008/06/23_veterans.shtml.

Armstrong, S., and Pruett, K. (2009, July). *From combat to career services: The role of university career counselors in serving our nation's veterans*. Paper presented at the annual meeting of the National Career Development Association, St. Louis, MO.

Arora, D. (2008, September 28). Student veterans adapt to college life. *The Daily Californian* (online). Retrieved January 8, 2011, from www.dailycal.org/article/102743/student_veterans_adapt_to_college_life.

Associated Press. (2010, May 31). WVU tailors classes for military veterans. *Charleston Daily Mail* (online). Retrieved November 29, 2010, from www.dailymail.com/News/201005310274.

Astin, A. (1993a). An empirical typology of college students. *Journal of College Student Development, 34,* 36–46.

Astin, A. (1993b). *What matters in college? Four critical years revisited.* San Francisco: Jossey-Bass.

Astin, A.W. (1984). Student involvement: A developmental theory for higher education. *Journal of College Student Personnel, 25,* 297–308.

Auburn University Veterans Task Force. (2010). Findings and recommendations from the Auburn University Veterans Task Force. *Auburn University* (online). Retrieved December 5, 2010, from www.auburn.edu/~diramdc/vtfreport.pdf.

Baechtold, M., and De Sawal, D. M. (2009). Meeting the needs of women veterans. *New Directions for Student Services, 126,* 35–43.

Bauman, M. C. (2009). *Called to serve: The military mobilization of undergraduates.* Unpublished doctoral dissertation, Pennsylvania State University. UMI No. 3380873.

Baxter Magolda, M. (1992). *Knowing and reasoning in college: Gender related patterns in students' intellectual development.* San Francisco: Jossey-Bass.

Baxter Magolda, M. B. (1999). *Creating contexts for learning: Constructive-developmental pedagogy.* Nashville: Vanderbilt University Press.

Baxter Magolda, M. B. (2007). Self-authorship: The foundation for twenty-first century education. *New Directions for Teaching and Learning, 109,* 69–83.

Baxter Magolda, M. B., and King, P. M. (2004). *Learning partnerships: Theory and models of practice to educate for self-authorship.* Sterling, VA: Stylus.

Beeson, M. J., and Wessel, R. D. (2002). The impact of working on campus on the academic persistence of freshmen. *NASFAA Journal of Student Financial Aid, 32*(2), 37–45.

Belenky, M., Clinchy, B., Goldberger, N., and Tarule, J. (1997). *Women's ways of knowing: The development of self, voice and mind* (10th anniversary ed.). New York: Basic Books.

Berger, J. B., and Milem, J. F. (1999). The role of student involvement and perceptions of integration in a causal model of student persistence. *Research in Higher Education, 40,* 641–664.

Bigelow, K. (Director). (2008). *The Hurt Locker* [Film]. Seattle: First Light Productions.

Biggs, S., Torres, S., and Washington, N. (1998). Minority student retention: A framework for discussion and decision making. *Negro Educational Review, 49,* 71–82.

Boldero, J., and Fallon, B. (1995). Adolescent help-seeking: What do they get help for and from whom? *Journal of Adolescence, 18,* 193–209.

Braxton, J. M. (2000). Introduction. In J. M. Braxton (Ed.), *Reworking the student departure puzzle* (pp. 1–8). Nashville: Vanderbilt University Press.

Braxton, J. M., Hirschy, A. S., and McClendon, S. A. (2004). *Understanding and reducing college student departure.* ASHE-ERIC Higher Education Report: 30(3). San Francisco: Jossey-Bass.

Braxton, J. M., and Lien, L. A. (2000). The viability of academic integration as a central construct in Tinto's interactionalist theory of student departure. In J. M. Braxton (Ed.), *Reworking the student departure puzzle* (pp. 11–28). Nashville: Vanderbilt University Press.

Braxton, J. M., and McClendon, S. A. (2001–2002). The fostering of social integration and retention through institutional practice. *Journal of College Student Retention, 3,* 57–72.

Braxton, J. M., and Mundy, M. E. (2001–2002). Powerful institutional levers to reduce college student departure. *Journal of College Student Retention, 3,* 91–118.

Braxton, J. M., Sullivan, A. S., and Johnson, R. (1997). Appraising Tinto's theory of college student departure. In J. Smart (Ed.), *Higher education: Handbook of theory and research* (Vol. 12, pp. 107–164). New York: Agathon.

Brenner, L. A., and others. (2008). A qualitative study of potential suicide risk factors in returning combat veterans. *Journal of Mental Health Counseling, 30*(3), 211–225.

Bridges, W. (2004). *Transitions: Making sense of life's changes.* Cambridge, MA: Da Capo Press.

Brokaw, T. (1998). *The greatest generation.* New York: Random House.

Brown, K. (2009, October 10). Veterans struggle to fit into college campuses. *National Public Radio* (online). Retrieved January 4, 2011, from www.npr.org/templates/story/story.php?storyId=113698227.

Burnett, S., and Segoria, J. (2009). Collaboration for military transition students from combat to college: It takes a community. *Journal of Postsecondary Education and Disability, 22*(1), 53–59.

Caffarella, R. S. (2002). *Planning programs for adults: A comprehensive guide* (2nd ed.). San Francisco: Jossey-Bass.

Chappell, B. (2010, November 4). Veterans who head to college lack support, study finds. *National Public Radio* (online). Retrieved January 3, 2011, from www.npr.org/blogs/thetwo-way/2010/11/04/131070705/support-is-lacking-for-veterans-who-head-to-college-study-finds.

Chase, S. E. (2005). Narrative inquiry: Multiple lenses, approaches, voices. In N. K. Denzin and Y. S. Lincoln (Eds.), *The Sage handbook of qualitative research* (3rd ed., pp. 651–679). Thousand Oaks, CA: Sage.

Chickering, A. W. (1969). *Education and identity.* San Francisco: Jossey-Bass.

Chickering, A. W., and Reisser, L. (1993). *Education and identity* (2nd ed.). San Francisco: Jossey-Bass.

Chickering, A. W., and Schlossberg, N. K. (2001). *Getting the most out of college* (2nd ed.). New York: Prentice Hall.

Church, T. E. (2009). Returning veterans on campus with war related injuries and the long road back home. *Journal of Postsecondary Education and Disability, 22*(1), 224–232.

Clark, B., and Trow, M. (1966). The organizational context. In T. Newcomb and E. Wilson (Eds.), *College peer groups: Problems and prospects for research* (pp. 17–70). Chicago: Aldine.

Cook, B. J., and Kim, Y. (2009). *From soldier to student: Easing the transition of service members on campus.* Washington, DC: American Council on Education.

Denzin, N. K. (2005). *Performance ethnography: Critical pedagogy and the politics of culture.* Thousand Oaks, CA: Sage.

DeSalvo, L. (1999). *Writing as a way of healing: How telling our stories transforms our lives.* Boston: Beacon Press.

Dey, E. L. (1997). Undergraduate political attitudes: Peer influence in changing social contexts. *Journal of Higher Education, 68*(4), 398–413.

Dinan, S. (2010, December 22). Obama signs bill to repeal 'don't ask, don't tell.' *Washington Times* (online). Retrieved January 9, 2011, from www.washingtontimes.com/news/2010/dec/22/obama-signs-dont-ask-dont-tell-repeal2/.

DiRamio, D., Ackerman, R. A., and Mitchell, R. L. (2008). From combat to campus: Voices of student veterans. *NASPA Journal, 45*(1), 73–102.

DiRamio, D., and Spires, M. (2009). Partnering to assist disabled veterans in transition. *New Directions for Student Services, 126,* 81–88.

Ely, M. B. (2008). Veterans in college: What advisers should expect. *The Mentor: An Academic Advising Journal, 10*(3), 1–2.

Epstein, J. (2009, October 22). Prerequisite: Experience in war. *Inside Higher Ed* (online). Retrieved December 5, 2010, from www.insidehighered.com/news/2009/10/22/veterans.

Erikson, E. (1968). *Identity: Youth and crisis.* New York: Horton.

Evans, N. J., and others. (2009). *Student development in college: Theory, research, and practice* (2nd ed.). San Francisco: Jossey-Bass.

Feldman, K. A., and Newcomb, T. M. (1969). *The impact of college on students.* San Francisco: Jossey-Bass.

Field, K. (2008, July 25). Cost, convenience drive veterans' college choices. *Chronicle of Higher Education, 54*(46), A1.

Fischer, F., and Miller, G. J. (Eds.). (2007). *Handbook of public policy analysis: Theory, politics, and methods.* Boca Raton, FL: CRC/Taylor & Francis.

Foster, L. K., and Vince, S. (2009). *California's women veterans: The challenges and needs of those who served.* California Research Bureau (online). Retrieved February 9, 2011, from www.library.ca.gov/crb/09/09-009.pdf.

Frankl, V. E. (2006). *Man's search for meaning.* Boston: Beacon Press.

Gaita, P. (2010, February 20). Scene dissection: Screenwriter Mark Boal breaks down *The Hurt Locker*'s most pivotal moments. *Los Angeles Times Online.* Retrieved December 18, 2010, from http://articles.latimes.com/2010/feb/20/entertainment/la-etw-boal20-2010feb20.

Gasendo, K. (2008, February 25). USC (University of Southern California) student veterans face limited resources. *Military Times* (online). Retrieved December 22, 2010, from www.militarytimes.com/forum/showthread.php?1562775-USC-%28University-of-Southern-California%29-student veterans-face-limited-resources.

Gettleman, J. (2005, September 10). After duty in Iraq, a new transition to being the non-fighting 69th. *New York Times* (online). Retrieved March 30, 2011 from http://www .nytimes.com/2005/09/10/nyregion/10dix.html.

Gilligan, C. (1981). Moral development in college years. In A. Chickering (Ed.), *The modern American college* (pp. 139–157). San Francisco: Jossey-Bass.

Gilligan, C. (1982). *In a different voice: Psychological theory and women's development.* Cambridge, MA: Harvard University Press.

Goldberger, N., Tarule, J., Clinchy, B, and Belenky, M. (Eds.). (1996). *Knowledge, difference, and power: Essays inspired by* Women's Ways of Knowing. New York: Basic Books.

Goodman, J., Schlossberg, N. K., and Anderson, M. L. (2006). *Counseling adults in transition: Linking practice with theory* (3rd ed.). New York: Springer.

Greenwood, P. E., and Nikulin, M. S. (1996). *A guide to chi-square testing.* New York: Wiley.

Grossman, P. D. (2009). Foreword with a challenge: Leading our campuses away from the perfect storm. *Journal of Postsecondary Education and Disability, 22*(1), 4–9.

Hackney, H., and Cormier, S. (2005). *The professional counselor: A process guide to helping* (5th ed.). Boston: Pearson.

Hall, L. K. (2008). *Counseling military families: What mental health professionals need to know.* New York: Routledge.

Hancock, L. (2007, March 23). College can be struggle for veterans. *Deseret Morning News* (online). Retrieved July 8, 2010, from findarticles.com/p/articles/mi_qn4188/ is_20070323/ ai_n18762643/.

Henderson, W. D. (2002). *Cohesion: The human element in combat.* Honolulu: University Press of the Pacific.

Herbert, M. S. (1998). *Camouflage isn't only for combat: Gender, sexuality, and women in the military.* New York: New York University Press.

Hoge, C. W. (2010). *Once a warrior, always a warrior: Navigating the transition from combat to home.* Guilford, CT: Globe Pequot Press.

Holloway, K. M. (2009). Understanding reentry of the modern-day student veteran through Vietnam-era theory. *Journal of Student Affairs, 18,* 11–17.

Holmstedt, K. A. (2009). *The girls come marching home: Stories of women warriors returning from the war in Iraq.* Mechanicsburg, PA: Stackpole Books.

Horowitz, H. L. (1987). *Campus life: Undergraduate cultures from the end of the eighteenth century to the present.* New York: Knopf.

Howe, N., and Strauss, W. (2000). *Millennials rising: The next great generation.* New York: Vintage Books.

Howell, D. C. (2002). *Statistical methods for psychology.* Pacific Grove, CA: Duxbury/ Thomson Learning.

Inks, M. (2009, April 14). More than words: Student profile (newsletter). *Department of English at West Virginia University* (online). Retrieved November 29, 2010, from english.wvu.edu/r/download/68280.

Jacobs, G. (2009, August 6). SDSU veterans house integrates vets into campus life. *SDSU News Center* (online). Retrieved January 18, 2011, from newscenter.sdsu.edu/sdsu_news-center/news.aspx?s=71472.

Johnson, J. (2010, November 4). Veterans who go back to school want more support. *Washington Post* (online). Retrieved June 14, 2011, from www.washingtonpost.com/wp-dyn/content/article/2010/11/03/AR2010110307448.html.

Johnson, T. (2009). Ensuring the success of deploying students: A campus view. *New Directions for Student Services, 126,* 55–60.

Jones, S., and McEwen, M. (2000). A conceptual model of multiple dimensions of identity. *Journal of College Student Development, 41,* 405–414.

Josselson, R. (1987). *Finding herself: Pathways to identity development in women.* San Francisco: Jossey-Bass.

Josselson, R. (1996). *Revising herself: The story of women's identity from college to midlife.* New York: Oxford University Press.

Junger, S. (2011). *War.* New York: Twelve Books/Hachette Book Group.

Kaberline, M. (2010, October 7). ASU recognized for helping veterans, families. *The Herald* (online). Retrieved November 28, 2010, from www.asuherald.com/news/asu-recognized-for-helping-veterans-families-1.2358743.

Kachigan, S. K. (1991). *Multivariate statistical analysis: A conceptual introduction.* New York: Radius.

Katchadourian, H., and Boli, J. (1985). *Careerism and intellectualism among college students: Patterns of academic and career choice in undergraduate years.* San Francisco: Jossey-Bass.

Kegan, R. (1994). *In over our heads: The mental demands of modern life.* Cambridge, MA: Harvard University Press.

Killough, A. C. (2009, June 1). Report outlines health concerns for student veterans. *Chronicle of Higher Education* (online). Retrieved December 16, 2010, from jobs.chronicle.com/article/Report-Outlines-Health/47675.

King, P. M. (2009). Principles of development and developmental change underlying theories of cognitive and moral development. *Journal of College Student Development, 50,* 597–620.

Klein, J. (2010, January 12). Back from war, bound for college. *New York Times Journalism Institute* (online). Retrieved December 1, 2010, from tucson10.nytimes-institute.com/2010/01/09/back-from-war-bound-for-college/.

Knowles, M. S., Holton, E. F., III, and Swanson, R. A. (2005). *The adult learner* (6th ed.). New York: Butterworth-Heinemann.

Kohlberg, L. (1969). Stage and sequence: The cognitive-developmental approach to socialization. In D. Goslin (Ed.), *Handbook of socialization theory and research.* Boston: Houghton Mifflin.

Kohlberg, L. (1984). *Essays on moral development: The psychology of moral development.* New York: HarperCollins.

Komiya, N., Good, G., and Sherrod, N. (2000). Emotional openness as a predictor of college students' attitudes. *Journal of Counseling Psychology. 47*(1), 138–143.

Kukla, A. (2000). *Social constructivism and the philosophy of science.* New York: Routledge.

Lattuca, L. R., and Stark, J. S. (2009). *Shaping the college curriculum: Academic plans in context* (2nd ed.). San Francisco: Jossey-Bass.

Lawson, J. (2010, April 12). Mission: College. What you need to know when you trade a rucksack for a book bag. *Military Times Edge* (online). Retrieved January 22, 2011, from www.militarytimesedge.com/education/veteran-campus-life/ed_combattocollege_040510w.

Lewin, K. (1936). *Principles of topological psychology.* New York: McGraw-Hill.

Lewis, P., and others. (2005). Identity development during the college years: Findings from the West Point Longitudinal Study. *Journal of College Student Development, 46*(4), 357–373.

Livingston, W. G. (2009). *Discovering the academic and social transitions of re-enrolling student veterans at one institution: A grounded theory.* Unpublished doctoral dissertation, Clemson University. UMI No. 3355150.

Llanos, C. (2010, May 16). CSUN sees increase in vets as grads. *Los Angeles Daily News* (online). Retrieved January 12, 2011, from www.dailynews.com/ci_15099521.

Looney, J., Robinson-Kurpius, S., and Lucart, L. (2004). Military leadership evaluations: Effects of evaluator sex, leader sex, and gender role attitudes. *Consulting Psychology Journal, 56,* 104–118.

Luft, J. (1969). *Of human interaction.* Palo Alto, CA: National Press Books.

Mangan, K. (2009, October 18). Colleges help veterans advance from combat to classroom. *Chronicle of Higher Education* (online). Retrieved July 9, 2010, from chronicle.com/article/Colleges-Help-Veterans-Advance/48846/.

Marcia, J. E. (1966). Development and validation of ego identity status. *Journal of Personality and Social Psychology 3,* 551–558.

Martinez, W. L., and Martinez, A. R. (2005). *Exploratory data analysis with MATLAB.* Boca Raton, FL: Chapman & Hall/CRC.

Maslow, A. H. (1954). *Motivation and personality.* New York: Harper & Brothers.

McEwen, M. K. (1996). New perspectives on identity development. In S. R. Komives and D. B. Woodard, Jr. (Eds.), *Student services: A handbook for the profession* (pp. 188–217). San Francisco: Jossey-Bass.

Merriam, S. B., Caffarella, R. S., and Baumgartner, L. M. (2007). *Learning in adulthood* (3rd ed.). San Francisco: Jossey-Bass.

Metz, G. W. (2004–2005). Challenge and changes to Tinto's persistence theory: A historical review. *Journal of College Student Retention, 6,* 191–207.

Milem, J. F. (1994). College, students, and racial understanding. *Thought and Action, 9*(2), 51–92.

Milem, J. F. (1998). Attitude change in college students: Examining the effect of college peer groups and faculty normative groups. *Journal of Higher Education, 69*(2), 117–140.

Mostafavi, B. (2011, January 21). Veteran of wars in Iraq and Afghanistan now championing student vets nationwide. *Flint Journal* (online). Retrieved February 10, 2011, from www.mlive.com/news/flint/index.ssf/2011/01/veteran_of_wars_in_iraq_and_af.html.

Myers, I. B., and McCaulley, M. H. (1985). *Manual: A guide to the development and use of the Myers-Briggs Type Indicator.* Palo Alto, CA: Consulting Psychologists Press.

National Academy of Sciences. (2008). Institute of Medicine: Long-term consequences of traumatic brain injury. *National Academies Press* (online). Retrieved February 1, 2011, from nap.edu/catalog/12436.html.

National Association of Colleges and Employers. (2010). *Job outlook 2010.* Bethlehem, PA: National Association of Colleges and Employers.

Newcomb, T., and Wilson, E. (1966). *College peer groups.* Chicago: Aldine.

New York Times. (2010, May 21). At war: Notes from the front lines. *New York Times, At War Blog* (online). Retrieved December 2, 2010, from atwar.blogs.nytimes.com.

Overman, S., and Leonard, B. (2010, June 27). Translating talent from military to civilian jobs. *Society for Human Resource Management* (online). Retrieved October 5, 2010, from www.shrm.org/about/news/Pages/MilitaryToCivilianJobs.aspx.

Pascarella, E. T., and Chapman, D. W. (1983). Validation of a theoretical model of college withdrawal: Interaction effects in a multi-institutional sample. *Research in Higher Education, 19,* 25–48.

Pascarella, E. T., and. Terenzini, P. T. (1991). *How college affects students: Findings and insights from twenty years of research.* San Francisco: Wiley.

Pascarella, E. T., and Terenzini, P. T. (2005). *How college affects students: A third decade of research.* San Francisco: Wiley.

Pearson, K. (1932). Experimental discussion of the (χ^2, P) test for goodness of fit. *Biometrika, 24,* 351–381.

Pennebaker, J. (2004). *Writing to heal: A guided journal for recovering from trauma and emotional upheaval.* Oakland, CA: New Harbinger Publications.

Perry, W. G. (1968). *Forms of intellectual and ethical development in the coming years: A scheme.* New York: Holt, Rinehart and Winston.

Perry, W. G. (1999). *Forms of ethical and intellectual development in the college years.* San Francisco: Jossey-Bass.

Persky, K. R. (2010). *Veterans education: Coming home to the community college classroom.* Unpublished doctoral dissertation, National-Louis University. Retrieved December 1, 2010, from digitalcommons.nl.edu/cgi/viewcontent.cgi?article=1031andcontext=diss.

Piaget, J. (1950). *The psychology of intelligence.* London: Routledge.

Pierce, P. (2006). The role of women in the military. In T. W. Britt, C. A. Castro, and A. B. Adler (Eds.), *Military life: The psychology of serving in peace and combat. Vol. 4. Military Culture* (pp. 97–118). Westport, CT: Praeger Security International.

Pizzalato, J. E. (2003). Developing self-authorship: Exploring the experiences of high-risk college students. *Journal of College Student Development, 44*(6), 797–812.

Public Law 103–160. (1993). *National Defense Authorization Act for Fiscal Year 1994.* Retrieved January 8, 2011, from www.law.cornell.edu/usc-cgi/get_external.cgi?type=pubLandtarget=103–160.

Rand Corporation. (2008). Invisible wounds: Mental health and cognitive care needs of America's returning veterans. *Rand Center for Military Health Policy Research* (online). Retrieved February 3, 2011, from http:// www.rand.org/pubs/research_briefs/RB9336.

Regus, E. (2008, August 14). Colleges reach out to vets. *The Press-Enterprise* (online). Retrieved January 6, 2011, from www.pe.com/localnews/inland/stories/PE_News_Local_S_veterans15.427d67a.html.

Rendón, L. (1994). Validating culturally diverse students: Toward a new model of learning and student development. *Innovative Higher Education, 19*, 33–51.

Rendón, L., Jalomo, R., and Nora, A. (2000). Theoretical considerations in the study of minority student retention in higher education. In J. Braxton (Ed.), *Rethinking the departure puzzle: New theory and research on college student retention* (pp. 127–156). Nashville: Vanderbilt University Press.

Rest, J., Narvaez, D., Bebeau, M. J., and Thoma, S. J. (1999). *Postconventional moral thinking: A neo-Kohlbergian approach.* Mahwah, NJ: Erlbaum.

Rhodes, F. (2001). *The creation of the future: The role of the American university.* Ithaca, NY: Cornell University Press.

Rosenheck, R. A., and Fontana, A. F. (2007). Recent trends in VA treatment of post-traumatic stress disorder and other mental disorders. *Health Affairs, 26*(6), 1720–1727.

Rumann, C. B., and Hamrick, F. A. (2010). Student veterans in transition: Re-enrolling after war zone deployments. *Journal of Higher Education, 81*(4), 431–458.

Sanford, N. (1966). *Self and society: Social change and individual development.* New York: Atherton Press.

Sanford, N. (1969). *Where colleges fail: A study of the student as a person.* San Francisco: Jossey-Bass.

Sax, L. J., Bryant, A. N., and Harper, C. E. (2005). The differential effects of student-faculty interaction on college outcomes for women and men. *Journal of College Student Development, 46*(6), 642–659.

Scharnberg, K. (2005, March 20). Stresses of battle hit female GIs hard: VA study hopes to find treatment for disorder. *Chicago Tribune*, p. 1.

Schlossberg, N. K. (1981). A model for analyzing human adaptation to transition. *Counseling Psychologist, 9*(2), 2–18.

Schlossberg, N. K. (1984). *Counseling adults in transition: Linking practice with theory.* New York: Springer.

Schlossberg, N.K. (1989). Marginality and mattering: Key issues in building community. *New Directions for Student Services, 48*, 5–15.

Schlossberg, N. K. (2004, June). *Transitions: Theory and applications.* Paper presented at the IAEVG-NCDA Symposium, San Francisco, CA.

Schlossberg, N. K. (2007). *Overwhelmed: Coping with life's ups and downs* (2nd ed.). New York: M. Evans.

Schlossberg, N. K., Lynch, A. Q., and Chickering, A. W. (1989). *Improving higher education environments for adults.* San Francisco: Jossey-Bass.

Schwandt, T. A. (2007). Literary turn (in social science) and Writing strategies [Dictionary entries]. *Sage dictionary of qualitative inquiry* (3rd ed., pp. 179–180, 322). Thousand Oaks, CA: Sage.

Science Daily. (2010, February 12). Many veterans not getting enough treatment for PTSD. *Science Daily* (online). Retrieved August 21, 2010, from www.sciencedaily.com/releases/2010/02/100210110742.htm.

Seal, K., and others. (2009). Trends and risk factors for mental health diagnoses among Iraq and Afghanistan veterans using Department of Veterans Affairs health care, 2002–2008. *American Journal of Public Health, 99,* 1651–1658.

Seaman, J. T. (2006). *A citizen of the world: The life of James Bryce.* New York: Tauris Academic Studies/Macmillan.

Servicemembers Opportunity Colleges. (2010). SOC Consortium Publications/Forms/Resources. *SOC* (online). Retrieved November 11, 2010, from www.soc.aascu.org/soc-consortium/PublicationsSOC.html.

Siebold, G. L. (2007). The essence of military group cohesion. *Armed Forces & Society, 33*(2), 286–295.

Sismour, E. (2010, November 11). Veterans and education: Are our veterans getting the education benefits they deserve? *Ezine Articles* (online). Retrieved February 4, 2011, from ezinearticles.com/?Veterans-and-Education:-Are-Our-Veterans-Getting-the-Education-Benefits-They-Deserve?andid=5367167.

Society of Human Resource Management. (2010). Employing military personnel and recruiting veterans. *SHRM* (online). Retrieved January 11, 2011, from www.shrm.org/Research/SurveyFindings/Documents/10-0531 Military Program Report_FNL.pdf.

Solaro, E. (2006). *Women in the line of fire: What you should know about women in the military.* Emeryville, CA: Seal Press.

State of Minnesota. (2010). Higher education veterans assistance program (197.585). *Minnesota Office of the Revisor of Statutes* (online). Retrieved January 11, 2011, from https://www.revisor.mn.gov/statutes/?id=197.585.

Sternberg, M., Wadsworth, S., Vaughan, J., and Carlson, R. (2009). *The higher education landscape for student service members and veterans in Indiana.* West Lafayette, IN: Military Family Research Institute at Purdue University. Retrieved September 16, 2010, from www.mfri.purdue.edu/content/Higher%20Education%20Landscape_web.pdf.

Sternberg, R. J., and Grigorenko, E. L. (2008). *Teaching for successful intelligence to increase student learning and achievement.* Thousand Oaks, CA: Corwin.

Stone, D. (2009, June 6). Love is a battlefield. *Newsweek* (online). Retrieved August 14, 2010, from www.newsweek.com/search.html?q=Love+Is+a+Battlefield.

Strauss, W., and Howe, N. (1991). *Generations: The history of America's future, 1584–2069.* New York: Morrow.

Strauss, W., and Howe, N. (2000). *Millennials rising: The next great generation.* New York: Vintage Books.

Student Veterans of America. (2010). About SVA. *Student Veterans of America* (online). Retrieved December 2, 2010, from www.studentveterans.org/about.

Summerlot, J., Green, S., and Parker, D. (2009). Student veterans organizations. *New Directions for Student Services, 126,* 71–79.

Tanielian, T., and Jaycox, L. (Eds.). (2008). *Invisible wounds of war: Psychological and cognitive injuries, their consequences, and services to assist recovery.* Santa Monica, CA: Rand Corporation.

Taylor, S. E., and others. (2000). Biobehavioral responses to stress in females: Tend-and-befriend, not fight-or-flight. *Psychological Review, 107,* 411–429.

Thompson, B. (2004). *Exploratory and confirmatory factor analysis: Understanding concepts and applications.* Washington, DC: American Psychological Association.

Tillo, C. (2011, January 7). Veterans return to college with a lot to adjust to. *Gainesville Sun* (online). Retrieved January 10, 2011, from www.gainesville.com/article/20110107/articles/110109630.

Tinto, V. (1975). Dropout from higher education: A theoretical synthesis of recent research. *Review of Educational Research, 45,* 89–125.

Tinto, V. (1993). *Leaving college: Rethinking the causes and cures of student attrition* (2nd ed.). Chicago: University of Chicago Press.

Tinto, V. (1997). Classrooms as communities: Exploring the educational character of student persistence. *Journal of Higher Education, 68,* 599–623.

Tinto, V. (2000). Linking learning and leaving. In J. M. Braxton (Ed.), *Reworking the departure puzzle* (pp. 81–24). Nashville: Vanderbilt University Press.

Toennies, F. (1957). *Community and society.* East Lansing: Michigan State University Press.

Torres, V., Jones, S. R., and Renn, K. A. (2009). Identity development theories in student affairs: Origins, current status, and new approaches. *Journal of College Student Development, 50,* 577–596.

Turner, R. H. (1990). Role change. *Annual Review of Sociology, 16*(1), 87–110.

Ulmer, W. F., and others. (2000). *American military culture in the twenty-first century: A report of the CSIS International Security Program.* Washington, DC: Center for Strategic and International Studies.

U.S. Department of Defense. (2009a). Population representation in the military service (FY 2009): Active component enlisted accessions by age, marital status, and gender with civilian comparison group. *U.S. Department of Defense* (online). Retrieved April 4, 2011, from prhome.defense.gov/MPP/ACCESSION%20POLICY/PopRep2009/appendixb/b_02.htm.

U.S. Department of Defense. (2009b). Population representation in the military service (FY 2009): Active component enlisted accessions by education tier, service, and race/ethnicity with civilian comparison group. *U.S. Department of Defense* (online). Retrieved April 4, 2011, from prhome.defense.gov/MPP/ACCESSION%20POLICY/PopRep2009/appendixb/b_07.htm.

U.S. Department of Education. (2010a). Central community college: Central to veteran student success grant. *Fund for the Improvement of Postsecondary Education* (online). Retrieved February 2, 2011, from http://fipsedatabase.ed.gov/grantshow.cfm?grantNumber= P116G100184.

U.S. Department of Education. (2010b). Veterans Upward Bound program. *U.S. Department of Education* (online). Retrieved April 26, 2011, from www2.ed.gov/programs/triovub/index.html.

U.S. Department of Veterans Affairs. (2008). The Post-9/11 Veterans Education Assistance Act of 2008. *VA Web site.* Retrieved September 23, 2010, from www.gibill.va.gov.

U.S. Department of Veterans Affairs (2009a, June 5). *Over 700 schools partner with VA to help veterans pay for education.* Retrieved July 22, 2010, from http://www1.va.gov/opa/pressrel/pressrelease.cfm?id=1694.

U.S. Department of Veterans Affairs. (2009b). Student work-study allowance program. *Veterans Administration* (online). Retrieved December 2, 2010, from www.gibill.va.gov/pamphlets/wkstud.htm.

U.S. Department of Veterans Affairs. (2009c). Yellow Ribbon program. *Veterans Administration* (online). Retrieved August 23, 2010, from www.gibill.va.gov/gi_bill_info/ch33/yellow_ribbon.htm.

U.S. Department of Veterans Affairs. (2010). VA announces expansion of VetSuccess on campus pilots. *Veterans Administration* (online). Retrieved January 11, 2011, from www1.va.gov/opa/pressrel/pressrelease.cfm?id=1978.

U.S. Department of Veterans Affairs. (2011). Military sexual trauma: Articles and fact sheets. *VA-Mental Health* (online). Retrieved February 21, 2011, from www.mentalhealth.va.gov/msthome.asp.

University of Arizona. (2010). AED 210: Resiliency and Human Potential (syllabus). *SERV— Transition Courses for Veterans* (online). Retrieved February 3, 2011, from vets.arizona.edu/documents/Syll_Resiliency_Fall09.pdf.

Valpar International Corporation. (2011). Aviator skills and interest assessment. *Valpar International Corporation* (online). Retrieved April 11, 2011, from www.valparint.com/aviator.htm.

Veteran Student Alliance at Sierra College. (2010). Mission statement. *Sierra College* (online). Retrieved October 19, 2010, from www.sierracollege.edu/studentservices/campusLife-ASSC/clubs/vetalliance/index.html.

Vygotsky, L. S. (1978). *Mind in society: The development of higher psychological processes.* Cambridge, MA: Harvard University Press.

Walker, C. (2010, November 20). War veteran barred from CCBC campus for frank words on killing. *Baltimore Sun* (online). Retrieved February 11, 2011 from http://articles.baltimoresun.com/2010-11-20/news/bs-md-veteran-suspension-20101121_1_iraq-veteran-war-veteran-campus-violence.

Wapner, S. (1981). Transactions of persons-in-environments: Some critical transitions. *Journal of Environmental Psychology, 1,* 223–239.

Washington State Legislature. (2011). SB 5608: Increasing assistance for student veterans at institutions of higher education. *Washington State Legislature* (online). Retrieved February 17, 2011, from apps.leg.wa.gov/billinfo/summary.aspx?bill=5608.

Weiss, R. S. (1975). *Marital separation.* New York: Basic Books.

Weiss, R. S. (1976). Transition states and other stressful situations: Their nature and programs for their management. In G. Caplan and M. Killilea (Eds.), *Support systems and mutual help: Multidisciplinary explorations* (pp. 17–26). New York: Grune & Stratton.

Widick, C., Parker, C. A., and Knefelkamp, L. (1978). Erik Erikson and psychosocial development. In L. Knefelkamp, C. Widick, and C. A. Parker (Eds.), *Applying new developmental findings*. New Directions for Student Services (No. 4, pp. 1–17). San Francisco: Jossey-Bass.

Winslow, D. (1998). Misplaced loyalties: The role of military culture in the breakdown of discipline in peace operations. *Canadian Review of Sociology and Anthropology, 35*(3), 345–367.

Woodrell, D. (2006). *Winter's bone.* New York: Little, Brown.

Yale University. (2010). Yale-led study to examine post-combat trauma among women veterans. *Daily Bulletin* (online). Retrieved April 26, 2011, from dailybulletin.yale.edu/article_print.aspx?id=7992.

Zaleznik, A., and Jardim, A. (1967). Management. In P. F. Lararsfeld, W. H. Sewell, and H. L. Wilensky (Eds.), *The uses of sociology* (pp. 193–234). New York: Basic Books.

Zoschke, N. (2010, October 11). Student veterans organization helps student veterans adjust to college life. *University News* (online). Retrieved January 7, 2011, from unews.com/2010/10/11/student veterans-organization-helps-student veterans-adjust-to-college-life.

Name Index

A

Abes, E. S., 57
Ackerman, R., 10, 13, 24, 25–26, 29, 35, 36, 38, 40, 62
Allen, D., 35
Alvarez, L., 22, 29
Ambrose, S. E., 27
American Council on Education (ACE), 1, 6, 10, 104, 110
Amy, L. E., 86
Anderson, M. L., 10, 17
Antonio, A. L., 21, 25, 29, 32
Anwar, Y., 85
Armstrong, S., 47
Arora, D., 53, 59
Associated Press, 85
Astin, A. W., 2, 4, 21, 22, 23, 24, 25, 28, 29, 30, 31, 32–33, 52, 61, 114
Auburn University Veterans Task Force, 21

B

Baechtold, M., 5, 71, 78, 79–80
Bauman, M. C., 36
Baumgartner, L. M., 16
Baxter Magolda, M. B., 2, 5–6, 55, 83, 86, 87, 88, 89
Bebeau, M. J., 89
Beeson, M. J., 52
Belenky, M., 76, 86
Berger, J. B., 35, 65
Bigelow, K., 7–8, 17, 28
Biggs, S., 48

Boal, M., 7
Boldero, J., 77
Boli, J., 61
Braxton, J. M., 2, 5, 35, 36, 41, 42, 44, 46, 47, 51–52, 107, 114
Brenner, L. A., 7
Bridges, W., 4, 8–9
Brokaw, T., 3
Brown, K., 64
Bryant, A. N., 78–79
Bryce, J., 6
Burnett, S., 40

C

Caffarella, R. S., 16
Carlson, R., 104
Chapman, D. W., 35
Chappell, B., 64
Chase, S. E., 8
Chickering, A. W., 2, 5, 25, 27, 28, 54, 56, 57, 64, 65, 66, 88–89
Church, T. E., 110
Clark, B., 61
Clinchy, B., 76, 86
Cook, B. J., 6, 10–11, 16, 95, 102, 112
Cormier, S., 16

D

Dakduk, M., 21
De Sawal, D. M., 71, 78, 79
Denzin, N. K., 8
DeSalvo, L., 82

Livingston, W. G., 36
Llanos, C., 84
Looney, J., 72
Lucart, L., 72
Luft, J., 59, 72
Lynch, A. Q., 57, 65

M
Mangan, K., 64
Marcia, J. E., 5, 59, 63, 64
Martinez, A. R., 96
Martinez, W. L., 96
McCaulley, M. H., 61
McClendon, S. A., 35, 47, 52
McEwen, M. K., 5, 30, 57, 59
Merriam, S. B., 16
Metz, G. W., 36
Milem, J. F., 21, 24, 25, 28, 35, 65
Miller, G. J., 96
Mitchell, R. L., 10, 13, 25–26, 29, 35, 38, 40
Mostafavi, B., 31
Mundy, M. E., 44
Myers, I. B., 61

N
Narvaez, D., 89
National Academy of Sciences, 110
National Association of Colleges and Employers, 48
New York Times, 29
Newcomb, T., 24
Newcomb, T. M., 24
Nikulin, M. S., 100
Nora, A., 48

O
Overman, S., 44

P
Parker, C. A., 65
Parker, D., 15–16, 42
Pascarella, E. T., 24, 31, 32, 35, 52
Pearson, K., 100
Pennebaker, J., 82

Perry, J., 55
Perry, W. G., 5, 83, 86, 89
Persky, K. R., 104
Piaget, J., 86, 87, 88
Pierce, P., 70
Pizzalato, J. E., 5–6, 83, 86, 87
Profit, G., 44
Pruett, K., 47

R
Rand Corporation, 110
Regus, E., 85
Reisser, L., 5, 28, 64, 66–67, 88–89
Rendón, L., 48, 76–77
Renn, K. A., 57, 60
Renner, J., 7
Rest, J., 89
Rhodes, F., 46
Robinson-Kurpius, S., 72
Rosenheck, R. A., 39
Rumann, C. B., 28, 35, 82

S
Sanford, N., 22–23
Sax, L. J., 78–79
Scharnberg, K., 70
Schlossberg, N. K., 2, 4, 9, 10, 11–12, 16, 18–19, 57, 65, 77, 89, 115
Schwandt, T. A., 8
Science Daily, 39
Seal, K., 38
Seaman, J. T., 6
Segoria, J., 40
Servicemembers Opportunity Colleges, 104
Sherrod, N., 77, 78
Siebold, G. L., 24
Sismour, E., 24
Society of Human Resource Management, 44
Solaro, E., 70
Spires, M., 8, 42
Stark, J. S., 86
State of Minnesota, 111
Sternberg, R. J., 88, 104
Stone, D., 28
Strauss, W., 3

Student Veterans of America (SVA), 31
Sullivan, A. S., 36, 46, 47
Summerlot, J., 15–16, 42
Swanson, R. A., 16

T

Tanielian, T., 16, 38
Tarule, J., 76, 86
Taylor, S. E., 77
Terenzini, P. T, 24, 31, 32, 52
Thoma, S. J., 89
Thompson, B., 96
Tillo, C., 57, 74
Tinto, V., 2, 4, 35, 42, 44, 46, 48, 63, 65
Toennies, F., 53
Torres, S., 48
Torres, V., 57, 60
Trow, M., 61
Turner, R. H., 13

U

Ulmer, W. F., 83, 86
University of Arizona, 84
U.S. Department of Defense, 23
U.S. Department of Education, 23–24, 30
U.S. Department of Veterans Affairs, 14, 36, 71, 107

V

Valpar International Corporation, 13
Vaughn, J., 104
Veteran Student Alliance, Sierra College, 27
Vince, S., 69, 70, 71, 73
von Braun, W., 115
Vygotsky, L. S., 86

W

Wadsworth, S., 104
Walker, C., 81, 82
Wapner, S., 4, 9
Washington, N., 48
Washington State Legislature, 111
Weiss, R. S., 18
Wessel, R. D., 52
Widick, C., 65
Wilson, E., 24
Winslow, D., 53
Woodrell, D., 69

Y

Yale University, 71

Z

Zaleznik, A., 12
Zoschke, N., 25

Subject Index

A

Academic advising services, 108
Academic and social integration, 44–50; with campus community, 46–47; critics of, 48–50
Administrative and strategic planning, 105–106
Affiliation, attainment of, 26
Ambivalent typology, 62
American Council on Education (ACE), 95
Anticipated transition, 10
Attributes: preentry, 36–40; and transition, 36–37
Authoring Your Life (Baxter Magolda), 92
Autonomy, moving toward interdependence, 67
Aviator (Valpar International Corporation), 13

B

Barriers to transition, 40
Beginnings and endings, 8–9
Belonging, attainment of, 26
Benefits, educational, 35, 38; processing of, 10; U.S. Department of Veterans Affairs, 14
Bond, military, 21–22
Bureaucratic red tape, and receipt of education benefits, 38

C

Campus life, encouraging involvement in, 24
Career services, 47–48

Chi-square analysis, 100
Cognitive development, 55
College student development, 5
Concept mapping, for curriculum planning, 86–89
Connectedness, 21–22
Cooperative Institutional Research Program survey, 61–62
Cramer's *V* coefficient, 100–101
Curriculum planning: concept mapping for, 86–89; introduction to self-authorship, 88–89; moral development, exploring, 89; orientation portion of course, 87–88; reflective writing, 88

D

Defining Issues Test (Rest), 89
Department of Defense, transition program (TAPS), 15
Departure puzzle, 41
Disabilities, 2, 39, 107, 110, 115
Disenchantment, 9
Disengagement, 8–9
Disidentification, 9
Disorientation, 9
"Don't ask, don't tell" policy, 60

E

Education and Identity (Chickering), 5
EFA Factor Five (Veterans Office on Campus), 111

EFA Factor Four (Psychological Counseling Services), 107–110
EFA Factor One (Financial Matters), 101–105
EFA Factor Three (Advising and Career Services), 105–107
EFA Factor Two (Administrative and Strategic Planning), 105–106
Emerging typology, 63–64
Emotions, managing, 66
Endings and beginnings, 8–9; neutral zone between, 9
Exploratory factor analysis (EFA), 96
External commitments, 41

F

Faculty training, 67
Female veterans, 5, 69–80; care/responsibility for others, sense of, 73–75; gender and assumptions, 72–73; help-seeking strategies, 77–78; history of, 69–70; as Identity Achievers, 79; and identity development, 79; learning to cope, 77–78; and military sexual trauma (MST), 71–72, 78; moral decision making, 75; number of women in military, 70–71; and PTSD, 71–72, 78; public view of women in combat, 70; sexual assault/harassment, 71; transition to civilian life, 73; voice, developing, 75–77
4S model (Schlossberg), 11–17; adaptation of, 12–13; changing of roles, 12–13; defined, 12
"Frog pond effect," 32
From Soldier to Student: Easing the Transition of Service Members on Campus (Cook/Kim), 6, 10–11, 95–97, 112
Fulfilled civilian self typology, 64–65

G

Gemeinschaft, 53
GI bill, 2–3; post-9/11, 14, 38
Goal commitment, 40–41; strength of, 41
Goodness of fit, in military, 53
Group norms, accommodation of, 53

H

Hard Facts, Dangerous Half-Truths and Total Nonsense (Pfeffer/Sutton), 9
Helping professionals: group meetings with that trend significant others, establishing, 19; one-to-one support system, 18; and role-change evaluation, 14; role of, 17; and transition, 8–9; weekly group meetings, 18–19
Hurt Locker, The (Bigelow), 7–8, 17, 28, 113

I

I-E-O model (Astin), 2, 22, 29; environmental factors, 23–24; inputs, 22–23; outcomes, 24–25; and veterans, 25–27
I-E-O-v model for veterans, 29–31; defined, 25
Identity crisis, 29, 53–67; identity formation theory, 59; multiple dimensions of identity, 59–61; multiple roles/ intersecting identities, 56–59; self-regulation and transition, 56; social construction of identity, 60–61; and student veterans, 53–67; typologies, 61–65
Identity development, 67; in early-career West Point cadets, 55; and self-knowledge, 54–55
Information-seeking behavior, encouraging, 16–17
Initial institutional experiences, 41–43
Injuries, 115
Institutional commitment, 41
Instruction delivery via the Internet, 115
Integrity, development of, 56

L

Learning partnerships, 92–93
Lumina Foundation for Education, 95

M

Man's Search for Meaning (Frankl), 84
Maryland community college case, 82
Maslow's hierarchy of needs, adaptation for student veterans, 26–27
Matriculation, 4

persistence, 43, 51–52; retuning expectations of, 86; scenarios for use with, 83; services provided to, by colleges and universities, 10–11; social development/academic integration of, 45; and transition, 7–19; women/female, *See* Female veterans
Student Veterans of America (SVA), 31

T

T1 (time one) institutional experiences/activities, 42–43
Tandem-bike metaphor, for learning partnerships, 93
Tinto's model of student departures, 36–37
Tinto's transition model, 35–52, 48; academic and social integration, 44–50; career services, 47–48; intent to persist, 48; new goals, 48; T1 (time one) institutional experiences/activities, 35–52
Transition, 7–19; assessment tools, 13–14; assistance, providing, 114; barriers to, 40; challenge of, 7; college attendance, 8; context in which transition occurs, 9–10; endings and beginnings, 8–9; equation, 11; goals and commitments, 40–41; helping professional, 8–9; identifying the type of transition, 10; initial institutional experiences, 41–43; model supporting (4S model), 11–17; and preentry attributes, 36–40; and self-regulation, 56; strategies, 16–17; Tinto's transition model, 35–52
Transition assessment tools, 13–14; institutional assistance, 16; stressful situations, 14–15
Typologies, 61–65; ambivalent, 62; emerging, 63–64; fulfilled civilian self, 64–65; skeptic, 62–63

U

Unanticipated transition, 10
Unified self, 59
University of Arizona, veteran-only courses, 84
University of California, Berkeley, Veterans in Higher Education, 85
University of Notre Dame, deployment polices, 104
U.S. Department of Veterans Affairs, 36; educational benefits, 14; VetSuccess program, 110

V

Veteran services, one-stop shop approach to, 114
Veterans, *see also* Female veterans; Student veterans: collegiate journey of, 4; educational benefits earned, 1; helping to find each other, 67; and I-E-O model (Astin), 25–27; institutional response to an emerging population of, 6, 95–112; transition from military duty to civilian college student, 4, 7–19
Veterans Administration, 15
Veterans in Higher Education course, UC, Berkeley, 85
Veterans Office on campus, 111
Veterans Upward Bound (VUB) program, 30

W

West Virginia University, veteran-only sections, 84–85
Winter's Bone (Woodrell), 69, 74
Women veterans, *See* Female veterans
Wounded Warrior programs, 74
Writing as a Way of Healing (DeSalvo), 82
Writing, reflective, 88

Y

Yellow Ribbon program, 106, 110

About the Authors

David DiRamio is an associate professor of higher education administration at Auburn University. DiRamio has written numerous publications, including a frequently cited article about issues facing this generation of veterans who are attending college and a book on how campuses can help student veterans succeed. DiRamio serves as the faculty advisor for Auburn University's Veterans Learning Community, an initiative for students with military experience to take classes with other student veterans who share similar interests and experiences. He serves as the National Association of Student Personnel Administrators' liaison for the American Council on Education's Severely Injured Military Veterans: Fulfilling Their Dream initiative, a program to assist severely injured veterans transition to college. DiRamio is the recipient of NASPA's 2006 Melvene Hardee Dissertation of the Year award. He received both B.S. and M.B.A. degrees from the State University of New York at Buffalo and a Ph.D. in educational leadership from the University of Nevada, Las Vegas. DiRamio is a U.S. Navy veteran.

Kathryn Jarvis has been an administrator and faculty member in private and public higher education for more than thirty years. She has written and presented in her fields nationally and internationally and most recently served as a member of the National Academic Advising Association journal editorial board. At Auburn University, she is responsible for academic support services, which include tutoring services, academic counseling, and freshman year courses. The text for the freshman-year course Success Strategies, which she edited, has been used by other colleges that offer similar programs. Jarvis teaches college student development in Auburn University's higher education graduate program. She served as the first dean of the faculty and acting president at Beacon College, where she was responsible for the leadership and management of a small college for students with learning disabilities. She previously taught undergraduate and graduate courses at Curry College and Lesley Graduate School of Education. Jarvis received a Ph.D. in higher education from Florida State University, an M.A. in education/child development from Tufts University, and a B.A. in communication disorders from the University of Florida.

About the ASHE Higher Education Report Series

Since 1983, the ASHE (formerly ASHE-ERIC) Higher Education Report Series has been providing researchers, scholars, and practitioners with timely and substantive information on the critical issues facing higher education. Each monograph presents a definitive analysis of a higher education problem or issue, based on a thorough synthesis of significant literature and institutional experiences. Topics range from planning to diversity and multiculturalism, to performance indicators, to curricular innovations. The mission of the Series is to link the best of higher education research and practice to inform decision making and policy. The reports connect conventional wisdom with research and are designed to help busy individuals keep up with the higher education literature. Authors are scholars and practitioners in the academic community. Each report includes an executive summary, review of the pertinent literature, descriptions of effective educational practices, and a summary of key issues to keep in mind to improve educational policies and practice.

The Series is one of the most peer reviewed in higher education. A National Advisory Board made up of ASHE members reviews proposals. A National Review Board of ASHE scholars and practitioners reviews completed manuscripts. Six monographs are published each year and they are approximately 120 pages in length. The reports are widely disseminated through Jossey-Bass and John Wiley & Sons, and they are available online to subscribing institutions through Wiley InterScience (http://www.interscience.wiley.com).

Call for Proposals

The ASHE Higher Education Report Series is actively looking for proposals. We encourage you to contact one of the editors, Dr. Kelly Ward (kaward@wsu.edu) or Dr. Lisa Wolf-Wendel (lwolf@ku.edu), with your ideas.

Recent Titles

ASHE HIGHER EDUCATION REPORT

ORDER FORM SUBSCRIPTION AND SINGLE ISSUES

DISCOUNTED BACK ISSUES:

Use this form to receive 20% off all back issues of *ASHE Higher Education Report*.
All single issues priced at **$23.20** (normally $29.00)

TITLE	ISSUE NO.	ISBN
_____	_____	_____
_____	_____	_____
_____	_____	_____

Call 888-378-2537 or see mailing instructions below. When calling, mention the promotional code JBNND to receive your discount. For a complete list of issues, please visit www.josseybass.com/go/aehe

SUBSCRIPTIONS: (1 YEAR, 6 ISSUES)

☐ New Order   ☐ Renewal

U.S.	☐ Individual: $174	☐ Institutional: $265
CANADA/MEXICO	☐ Individual: $174	☐ Institutional: $325
ALL OTHERS	☐ Individual: $210	☐ Institutional: $376

Call 888-378-2537 or see mailing and pricing instructions below.
Online subscriptions are available at www.onlinelibrary.wiley.com

ORDER TOTALS:

Issue / Subscription Amount: $ _____

Shipping Amount: $ _____
(for single issues only – subscription prices include shipping)

Total Amount: $ _____

SHIPPING CHARGES:
First Item $5.00
Each Add'l Item $3.00

(No sales tax for U.S. subscriptions. Canadian residents, add GST for subscription orders. Individual rate subscriptions must be paid by personal check or credit card. Individual rate subscriptions may not be resold as library copies.)

BILLING & SHIPPING INFORMATION:

☐ **PAYMENT ENCLOSED:** *(U.S. check or money order only. All payments must be in U.S. dollars.)*

☐ **CREDIT CARD:**   ☐ VISA   ☐ MC   ☐ AMEX

Card number _____ Exp. Date _____

Card Holder Name_____ Card Issue # _____

Signature _____ Day Phone_____

☐ **BILL ME:** *(U.S. institutional orders only. Purchase order required.)*

Purchase order # _____
Federal Tax ID 13559302 • GST 89102-8052

Name_____

Address_____

Phone_____ E-mail_____

Copy or detach page and send to: **John Wiley & Sons, PTSC, 5th Floor**
989 Market Street, San Francisco, CA 94103-1741

Order Form can also be faxed to: **888-481-2665**

PROMO JBNND

ENABLE
DISCOVERY

Introducing WILEY ONLINE LIBRARY

Wiley Online Library is the next-generation content platform founded on the latest technology and designed with extensive input from the global scholarly community. Wiley Online Library offers seamless integration of must-have content into a new, flexible, and easy-to-use research environment.

Featuring a streamlined interface, the new online service combines intuitive navigation, enhanced discoverability, an expanded range of functionalities, and a wide array of personalization options.